A Cultural History of Jews in California

The Jewish Role in American Life

An Annual Review

A Cultural History of Jews in California

The Jewish Role in American Life

An Annual Review

Volume 7

Bruce Zuckerman, *Editor*
William Deverell, *Guest Editor*
Lisa Ansell, *Associate Editor*

Published by the Purdue University Press for
the USC Casden Institute for the Study of the
Jewish Role in American Life

© 2009 by the
University of Southern California
Casden Institute for the
Study of the Jewish Role in American Life.
All rights reserved.

Production Editor, Marilyn Lundberg

Cover photo:
Isaias Hellman in San Francisco, c. 1890s.
Photographer unknown. Collection of Christiane de Bord.

ISBN 978-1-55753-564-1
ISSN 1934-7529

Published by Purdue University Press
West Lafayette, Indiana
www.thepress.purdue.edu
pupress@purdue.edu

Printed in the United States of America.

For subscription information,
call 1-800-247-6553

Contents

FOREWORD — vii

EDITORIAL INTRODUCTION — xi

Frances Dinkelspiel — 1
Isaias Hellman and the Creation of California

Karen S. Wilson — 25
A Twice-Told Journey: Sarah Newmark in the
Russian Polish Shtetl—How a Jewish California
Matron Confronted Her European Heritage

Gladys Sturman and David Epstein — 47
Postscript: The Western States Jewish History Archives

Shana Bernstein — 55
From Civic Defense to Civil Rights: The Growth
of Jewish American Interracial Civil Rights
Activism in Los Angeles

Gina Nahai — 81
The Third Temple: Iranian Jews and the
Blessings of Exile—A Personal Memoir

Marsha Kinder — 95
Jewish Homegrown History: In the Golden
State and Beyond

ABOUT THE CONTRIBUTORS — 125

ABOUT THE USC CASDEN INSTITUTE — 127

Foreword

Beginning with our previous volume of the Casden *Annual Review* (Volume 6), the annual publication of the Casden Institute for the Study of the Jewish Role in American Life, the editors decided to focus on a single topic and to present articles that largely consider aspects of that topic alone. That volume, subtitled, *The Impact of the Holocaust in America*, was very well received and gave us the opportunity to explore an area of Shoah-studies that had not been well emphasized previously. With this volume (Volume 7), we continue this policy of focusing on a single topic, but in this case the topic we have turned to is, quite literally, closer to home: the Jewish role in California life.

There are two aspects of this volume that merit special notice. First, the aim of the collection of essays and studies in this volume is intended to stress the *cultural* aspects of the Jewish experience of coming to and living in the Golden State. We cannot hope to present in this limited venue a comprehensive and detailed history of how Jews came to live in California, *per se*. Rather, it is our more limited goal to consider a number of insightful perspectives on how the Jews, who settled in California, helped shape the Golden State's culture and were, in turn, themselves molded by cultural influences that were uniquely Californian. Second, while this volume looks at the Jewish experience in California in general—nonetheless, particular emphasis is placed on *Southern California*. Both these concerns, of course, are natural ones for the Casden Institute to consider. First of all, the focus on California simply follows—although in more geographical detail—the overall mandate of the Casden Institute, to consider the special part that Jews have played in the culture of their adopted homeland. Moreover, it seems entirely appropriate that an institute that resides at the University of Southern California should look out at the Jewish role in this special state as seen from the perspective of this even more special, local neighborhood. After all, Jews played (and continue to play) a notable role in building and defining what Southern California is and, beyond this, what we imagine it to be. We firmly believe that there is something special about the Jewish role in California and even more so in Southern California—that here on the lower left-coast Jews have had an Americanization experience that is significantly different from that which Jews have experienced elsewhere in the USA. Conversely, Southern California would be quite a different place without the Jews who made it their home.

We begin our cultural history at a crucial moment in California history, the mid-nineteenth century in the after-glow of the California Gold Rush, where we encounter a European Jewish emigrant, fresh off the boat, who could (and did) get a chance to make a fortune in the pueblo of Los Angeles and, in doing so, helped define what California is. We conclude it with a personal meditation from one of the latest group of refugees to come to the west, the Iranian Jews who were forced out of their ancient homeland some thirty years ago and who found in Southern California a particularly hospitable (yet no less difficult) place to transplant their cultural roots. In between, we are treated to a few choice snapshots of how life developed and changed for Jews in California as California itself evolved and grew. But if this volume proves one thing for sure, it is this: that we have only just begun to scratch the surface of a rich but largely unknown cultural resource. At best, this volume can only give us a hint of what we have yet to learn.

The impetus for this *Annual Review* came in no small part from a grant that the Casden Institute gave to my professorial colleagues at USC, William Deverell and Marsha Kinder, who needed a little funding to facilitate their bringing together in an orderly and academic fashion some of the primary source material on the Jews who settled in California and especially the southern part of the state. One product of this highly successful research effort was a desire on their part to pull this volume together to serve as a showcase of what they and their colleagues have learned and what research opportunities they continue to pursue. Prof. Kinder, in an article at the conclusion of this volume, in particular, outlines an ambitious plan to develop a Jewish "homegrown history" that begins in California but intends to span the entire country. Prof. Deverell has taken on the special responsibilities of serving as guest editor for this volume, and he has managed this important task with great professionalism. I am particularly grateful to him for all the many hours of effort he has invested in making this volume something we are all quite proud of. I also wish to thank Associate Director of the Casden Institute, Lisa Ansell who, as Associate Editor of this volume, has done so many little things (and quite a few big things too!) to make this volume better and the Casden Institute better. My longtime associate Marilyn J. Lundberg, production editor for this volume, has brought everything together with her usual, awesome efficiency. Both Lisa and Marilyn not only made this volume possible, but each of them has invested considerable effort into keeping my life from becoming impossible.

Special thanks also goes to Howard Gillman, the Dean of the College of Letters Arts & Sciences and C. L. Max Nikias, Provost, for their continuing vision for the Casden Institute as an integral and vibrant part of USC. Susan Wilcox, Associate Dean for College Advancement continues to be my wisest of wise counselors. As of this writing, we have just learned that the longtime President of USC, Steven B. Sample, will be retiring in 2010. President Sample's support and enthusiasm for all aspects of research relevant to Jewish studies on our campus—from ancient times to modern times—has been a key factor to the advancement of the field at our university. As is the case for so many academic elements that make USC the great center of learning that it is ever becoming, the Casden Institute owes an enduring debt of gratitude to President Sample.

I reserve a final word for a few special people, who in many ways are the embodiment of what this volume of the Casden *Annual Review* is all about: Ruth Ziegler, Carmen Warschaw, Kenneth Leventhal, Stanley Gold and Alan Casden. Each one of them has been a major force at USC and in Southern California, not only for the advancement of Jewish Studies and the Casden Institute, but for the pursuit and advancement of excellence in our region and, indeed, in the world. We are all very fortunate that they, too, along with their families and loved ones, found their way to Southern California where they could build a life that is both distinctly Jewish and distinctly Californian.

It is insightful to note that I have always been asked by Alan Casden to use my full title—not just Director of the Casden Institute, but *Myron and Marion Casden* Director. Myron and Marion are Alan Casden's parents, and it is clear that he sees the pursuits of the Casden Institute as being a special homage to them—his way of acknowledging how much he owes his success to their efforts as Jews and Americans, to find a productive role in our country. Alan Casden's personal story is, in microcosm, a reflection of the greater story of the Jewish contribution to America (and especially to Southern California)—a story that in macrocosm merits the kind of academic recognition and careful study that this volume intends to represent. It therefore seems all the more appropriate to dedicate this volume to Alan Casden and his parents Myron and Marion Casden, whose role in the life of Southern California, America and the world is something for which those of us who were born and raised in Los Angeles can be most grateful.

Bruce Zuckerman, *Myron and Marian Casden Director*

Editorial Introduction

by William Deverell

Working on this volume of the Casden *Annual Review* has been a distinct pleasure. I've been able to renew friendships with a number of talented senior and junior scholars, and I've learned a great deal about an especially vibrant subfield of American and western American history. I am grateful to my colleagues Bruce Zuckerman, Myron and Marion Casden Director of the Casden Institute at USC, and Lisa Ansell, Associate Director of the Casden Institute, for the invitation to draw together these diverse essays on the subject of Jewish California. I'm especially grateful to my colleague Marsha Kinder; it was Marsha who first approached me several years ago to inquire whether I would care to become a partner on an intriguing multimedia and scholarly investigation of Jewish life and history in California and the far West. Having but a passing knowledge of this topic, and knowing of its importance to my field of interest (the American West generally), I was only too happy to become involved in the "Homegrown Jewish History" project which Marsha and Rosemary Comella have so expertly directed and put together. This project will be presented in detail Marsha's contribution to this volume.

Along the way, I've had the good fortune of working closely not only with my USC friends and colleagues, but with others as well. Frances Dinkelspiel, an old friend from long ago college days, contacted me several years ago so that we might talk about nineteenth-century California, especially as it related to her extraordinarily important great, great-grandfather, Isaias W. Hellman. After several years of diligent, careful research, Frances produced a superb biography of Hellman, a man whose own career and rise to banking and financial prominence is intricately interwoven with the state of California's own maturation and development. I'm pleased to have convinced Frances to contribute an essay to this volume drawn from her wonderful book.

Through my budding interest in Jewish California, I quickly encountered UCLA graduate student Karen Wilson, a doctoral candidate at work on a dissertation exploring the nineteenth-century Jewish history of Los Angeles. Talented, diligent, and extremely knowledgeable about her subject of interest, Karen has contributed two pieces to this Casden Annual; one is an examination of the continuing ties which pioneering Jews of California maintained with Europe in the turn-of-the-century period, a theme Karen develops more fully in her doctoral work. The other is a fine annotation of an important diary from the same period (and same family), a document now housed in the Huntington Library's collections.

That this document which Karen worked on has found a home in the Huntington is not simply a case of good archival luck. On the contrary, thanks to the deep devotion of Gladys Sturman and David Epstein to the history of Jews of the West, we are all the beneficiaries of decades and decades of collecting efforts. David and Gladys are the archival heirs to the important work of Rabbi William Kramer and Dr. Norton B. Stern; in their postscript essay to this volume, Sturman and Epstein sketch out the history of the Western States Jewish History collections which they have so carefully superintended (and organized and studied). Thanks to their real appreciation of the importance of these archives, the materials have been and are being transferred to research institutions across greater Los Angeles where they can be drawn more broadly into scholarly work and scholarly curiosity.

Lastly, pulling together this volume allowed me to (finally) get the chance to publish something from the work of talented young American historian Shana Bernstein. Her essay in this volume, about Jews and civil rights in Cold War California, is drawn from her important new book on the topic. She reminds us that the Jewish history of the far West is inextricably tied to issues of racial accommodation and fights for racial equity.

There is also a fine contribution by the talented novelist Gina Nahai, in which she chronicles in a highly personal manner her journey as an Iranian Jew to Southern California and through it a sense of what this experience meant and continues to mean for these newest Jewish immigrants to the southwest.

Taken together, these essays and contributions—themselves but the tip of a growing iceberg of inquiry—provide tantalizing hints of the body of sources "out there" awaiting scholarly questions and scholarly efforts. Thanks to the work of the contributors to this volume and others, we know quite a bit about the Jewish history of California and the West. But there is so much more to know.

Isaias Hellman and the Creation of California

Frances Dinkelspiel

On a spring evening in 1886, Harrison Gray Otis, a forty-nine year old Civil War veteran who was one of the co-owners of the *Los Angeles Daily Times*, made a courtesy call on Isaias Hellman, the president of Los Angeles' largest bank. Hellman was at home in his thirteen-room Italianate mansion that evening, not at his office at the Farmers and Merchants Bank, so Otis made his way to the corner of Fourth and Main Streets. The neighborhood, just three-quarters of mile southeast of the Plaza, had been one of Los Angeles' best since 1865, when former Governor John Downey and his wife Maria built the first brick mansion in the area. Hellman had constructed his own ornate home nearby in 1877, and the two-story house with large windows, a mansard roof, a wraparound porch, and walls frescoed with painted scenes of Germany, the Mississippi delta and the Arroyo Seco, was considered one of the nicest in the city (*Los Angeles Star*, Sept. 13, 1877).

The two men settled into Hellman's parlor. At forty-three, Hellman was a serious-looking man with a receding hairline, dark Van Dyke beard and large brown eyes that peered from behind gold rimmed glasses. As one of Los Angeles' richest men, he deferred to no one, and while this gave him a solemn air, it did not mean he was not curious to hear why his guest had called. Otis, on the other hand, with his white hair, bushy beard and Colonel's title, still had not fulfilled his dreams of journalistic glory and business success. He knew that this conversation with Hellman might set his future's course.

The two had little in common. Hellman, a cautious businessman, was a Jewish immigrant from Germany who had lived in Los Angeles for twenty-seven years. Otis had been born in Marion, Ohio to an abolitionist father and had lived an itinerant life, fighting for the Union Army under William McKinley, training as a printer in Kentucky and Washington, DC and only coming to Los Angeles in 1882 to take over as editor of the *Los Angeles Daily Times*. The paper was just eight months old at that point, but Otis had quickly seen its possibilities and within a brief period had gained control of half of the paper's assets.

Now Otis had a problem. He and his partner, Henry Harrison Boyce, were not getting along. Their disagreements about how to run the paper threatened to undo the business they had created. Boyce wanted to buy out Otis or sell his shares in the paper, and had set a tight deadline for a decision. But price was an issue. Boyce wanted the princely sum of $18,000. It was money that Otis did not have.

It had not been easy to turn a profit in the news business. Los Angeles was crowded with newspapers, each competing for a small segment of the town's approximately 20,000 residents. In addition to the *Times*, there was the *Daily Herald*, the *Evening Express*, and a smattering of smaller papers.

Yet there were signs that business was improving and Otis was determined to retain his association with the *Times*. During the last few years Los Angeles had been growing at a rapid rate. The Santa Fe Railroad had completed its transcontinental line the year before, giving the Southern Pacific Railroad its first competition since arriving in Los Angeles ten years earlier. The ensuing rate war was luring thousands of visitors a month, and many of them decided to stay permanently after they enjoyed the region's mild weather. The city's population had jumped from 11,000 to 20,000 in just the past six years.[1] Land sales had picked up considerably in the first few months of 1886 as realty and land companies set up for business. And the best place to advertise those plots of land? The newspapers, of course.

Hellman listened to Otis's story and realized that he and the newspaper man shared at least one thing in common: a belief in the future of Los Angeles. By the end of the evening Hellman had offered to loan Otis the full $18,000. It was a gesture of faith, and one that Otis would remember the rest of his life.

"I have never forgotten the pregnant interview which I had with you, in your own parlor, about March 1886, when the problem to be resolved was how to get full control of the paper and rescue it from impending ruin by a pretender and a scoundrel," Otis wrote Hellman years later. "Then it was that you said that wise thing, that it would be of no avail, in the long run, for you to help me unless that help was made sufficient to enable me to get control and tread the deck of the ship as its sure enough commander. That aid you rendered and then and there was the problem solved, the battle won. For all of which, believe me, I am your friend" (Otis, Letter to Hellman).

Hellman's loan let Otis acquire full ownership of the paper. Otis went on to become wealthy and to gain unprecedented influence in southern California. Over time, the *Los Angeles Times* became the most significant paper in the region. And when Otis needed additional capital to construct his new Times building, he turned to Hellman's Farmers and Merchants Bank for the funds.

The loan to Otis was only one of thousands Hellman made during his career as a banker, but it deftly illustrates how his financial acumen played a critical role in the growth of Los Angeles. Hellman had an uncanny ability to figure out which businesses might succeed and which businessmen to back. These instincts led him to take chances on companies that other banks would not touch—and were instrumental to the development of the state's economy. His judgment and access to capital transformed Hellman into the most influential financier on the Pacific Coast during the latter part of the nineteenth century and the early part of the twentieth century.

The period after the Civil War witnessed one of the largest economic expansions in US history. The chaotic markets and industrial boom of the era created a new class of capitalist, men who accumulated gargantuan fortunes in a relatively short time span. Men like Jacob Schiff and J. P. Morgan forged financial dynasties and networks that were in some ways more powerful than the central government. As the age of the independent financier evolved into the age of the corporation, those nineteenth-century titans helped lead the United States from being an agrarian-based economy to become an industrial dynamo.

Bankers in California were too far from the financial centers of New York, London, and Paris to equal the significance of their East Coast counterparts, but they were instrumental in helping transform California from an isolated outpost where capital was measured in animal hides and gold nuggets into an economic powerhouse driven by mining and agriculture interests.

In a time of unsophisticated financial markets, when banks minted their own money, bankers like Hellman were the men who smoothed over the rough edges of the economy. They offered credit, invested in companies, and issued instruments of debt. During financial panics—which happened roughly every ten years in the nineteenth century—Hellman and his fellow bankers provided an essential stability.

No banker was more critical to the growth of California than Isaias

Hellman. By the time of his death in 1920, he was president of Wells Fargo Bank and served as president or director of seventeen other banks.[2] He was a major investor and promoter of at least eight industries that shaped California—banking, transportation, education, land development, water, electricity, oil, and wine—lending money to jump start many of those industries.

"No one man in California has left an impress upon the financial affairs of the state in so many different communities and in such an unquestioned manner as I. W. Hellman," Ira Cross wrote in his four-volume *Financing an Empire: History of Banking in California* (539).

*****

Hellman first spotted the shores of Southern California from the deck of a steamer coming from San Francisco. It was May 14, 1859 and the port of San Pedro was nothing more than a collection of barracks scattered among the marshes on the shoreline. The water was so shallow that ocean-going ships could not dock, so Hellman, aged sixteen, and his traveling companion, his brother, Herman, fifteen, boarded a lighter to carry them to shore.

Los Angeles had only been part of the United States for nine years at that point, and it was a town in transition, a place slowly evolving from Mexican to American rule. While the Gold Rush had brought thousands of people to Northern California, transforming San Francisco almost overnight into a bustling city, Southern California was still a frontier community on the edge of the continent, difficult to get to and almost completely isolated.

Only 4,400 people lived in the town, with another 11,000 in the surrounding counties. There was no regularly scheduled stage coach from San Francisco or Salt Lake City, and steamers stopped at the port only a few times a month. There was no telegraph connection to San Francisco; news often took two weeks or more to reach the area. Both of the town's newspapers, the *Los Angeles Star* and *El Clamor Publico*, published articles in Spanish, although the *Star* also had an English edition. Most residents were illiterate. Spanish was the most widely spoken language, followed by French and then English. A self-selected volunteer group called the Rangers acted as a police force, and they answered to their own authority.

Hellman and his brother had left Reckendorf, a small town in Bavaria, to escape Germany's stringent restrictions on where Jews could live and what professions they could join. The Hellman brothers were part of a massive migration from central Europe that would triple the US Jewish population from 50,000 in 1850 to 150,000 by 1860. While most of those Jews would settle on the East Coast, a small number were lured to California by the promise of gold. By 1860, there were about 10,000 Jews living in California, with 5,000 settled in San Francisco and the rest scattered around the state (Benjamin 233).

Quite a number of Hellmans had found their way to Los Angeles, including Isaias Hellman's maternal uncle and four first cousins. No records remain that indicate why members of the family settled in southern California, but they may have had some acquaintance with Phillip Sichel, one of the eight Jewish men recorded in the 1850 census.[3] Hellman went to work as a clerk at Hellman & Brothers, a dry goods store on Mellus' Row owned by his cousins Isaiah M. and Samuel M. Hellman. In his early days, before he had mastered English, Hellman drove a wagon of goods around to the ranchos in the surrounding countryside (Mesmer 199). Within a short time, however, he was working behind the counter and offering advice to his cousins, an early indicator of his growing business savvy. "I. W. Hellman immediately showed much ability and greatly improved his cousin's business," Harris Newmark wrote in his memoirs (Newmark 248).

Hellman joined a small but cohesive Jewish community, but he also traveled easily among Yankees and the Californios, as those born in California when it was part of Mexico were known. From the start of the American era, Los Angeles was accommodating to its Jewish residents. While cities on the East Coast had a clearly delineated social hierarchy, California was still a state in transition, more interested in setting up city councils and police departments than excluding entire classes of citizens. Jews were part of the Los Angeles city fabric from its inception. Morris L. Goodman was elected to the first City Council in 1850, and Arnold Jacobi was elected in 1853 (Vorspan and Gartner 17). Another Jew, Maurice Kremer, was elected County Treasurer in 1859 (Vorspan and Gartner 18). Hellman's cousin, Isaiah M. Hellman, won the post of city treasurer in 1876 (*Los Angeles Daily Republican* Dec. 4, 1876: 2). Hellman and other Jews joined Masonic orders that were comprised of both Jews and Gentiles (Vorspan and Gartner 22). Hellman learned Spanish from the rector Francisco Mora (Engh 158), who would go on to serve as the Catholic Bishop of the Monterey-Los Angeles region (Dinkelspiel 30).

When Hellman arrived in 1859, he practiced a traditional form of Judaism, but that changed as he became more Americanized.[4] He was an early member of Congregation B'nai B'rith and served as president when the group erected the city's first synagogue in 1872 ("Hebrew Synagogue"). His wife, Esther Hellman, was a member of the Ladies Hebrew Benevolent Society (Dinkelspiel 59) and his son Marco was bar mitzvah in 1884 ("The Bar Mitzvah of a Banker's Son").

After working for his cousin for five years, Hellman set out on his own. In 1865, he bought a store on the southeast corner of Main and Commercial streets from Adolph Portugal, a Jewish merchant who was heading back to Europe ("Dry Goods"). Hellman sold clothes, hats and ribbons, and took frequent trips to San Francisco to find reasonably priced goods ("Dry Goods & Clothing Emporium"). In a concession to his new land, Hellman kept his store open on Saturdays, the Jewish Sabbath (Dinkelspiel 61).

As a service to customers, Hellman installed a $160 Tilden and McFarland safe in the back of his shop and offered to store gold and valuables (Ledger 1865). Banks were illegal in California at that time, so people often kept their money in the safes of trusted merchants (Dinkelspiel 42).

Hellman made informal bank transactions until he had a run-in with a bleary-eyed Irishman who had wandered in and out of his store over a week's time, always gloriously drunk and eager to take money out of his gold pouch. When the Irishman sobered up, he returned to Hellman's store and was furious to find that there was no money left. At first he accused Hellman of stealing the funds, but was convinced by a friend that no thievery had occurred. "What is to prevent one of those fellows from cracking me over the head, sticking a knife in my ribs, or shooting me?" Hellman recalled later in an interview (Cross 546). Nothing, he realized.

After nearly getting punched, Hellman changed the way he did business. Instead of storing a customer's gold, Hellman decided he would only buy it outright, deposit it in his safe, and give the customer a passbook to keep tracks of deposits and withdrawals. He asked a typesetter to print slips that said "I. W. Hellman, Banker."[5] It was the start of banking in Los Angeles.[6]

In 1868, Hellman joined forces with two Los Angeles pioneers to open a formal bank ("New Banking Enterprise"). They were William Workman and F. P. F. Temple, both part of the group of American settlers who had came to California when it belonged to Mexico and had married women with ties to the elite Californio class. It was an astute choice, for Workman and Temple were highly regarded in Los Angeles and provided an imprimatur of respectability on the bank and its twenty-six year old cashier. For the rest of his life, Hellman would forge partnerships with men more powerful than himself, both Jewish and Gentile.[7]

Hellman, Temple and Co. opened just a few months after former

California Governor John Downey had started a bank in partnership with James Hayward, son of a successful miner. By 1871, Hellman and Downey had dissolved their previous partnerships and had gone into business together (Dinkelspiel 70). They recruited twenty-three other prominent businessmen to sit on a board and opened the Farmers and Merchants Bank in April 1871 in a building on Main Street right next to the Bella Union Hotel. The group of men who founded and capitalized the bank were some of the wealthiest and most prominent in the city (Cleland and Putnam 19–24), and included Hellman's brother, Herman, who owned a large dry goods store, his cousin, Isaiah M. Hellman, a merchant, Ozro Childs, a wealthy horticulturist, James F. Burns, county sheriff, Matthew Keller, a vintner and landowner, Cameron Thom, the district attorney and future mayor, William Perry, a lumberman and president of the gas company, Jose Mascarel, a merchant, Domingo Amestoy, a livestock owner, and more. They were Jewish and Gentile. Only one group was noticeably missing: representatives from the old Californio elite. The absence reflected the sad reality that the group that once dominated California no longer commanded much power.

The creation of the Farmers and Merchants Bank, with a capitalization of $500,000 (Cleland and Putnam 25), proved critical to the development of Los Angeles. For the previous two decades money had only been available to borrow at very high interest rates, sometimes reaching as high as fifteen percent a month (Cleland and Putnam 17). Many Californios had lost their land because of these confiscatory interest rates. (Downey, in fact, was a beneficiary of the region's tight money supply. In one poignant example, in 1852 Downey lent $5,000 to Lemuel Carpenter who put up his 17,000 acre Rancho San Gertrudes as collateral. By 1859, compounded interest had increased the debt to $100,000 and a despairing Carpenter committed suicide. Downey then purchased the ranch at a sheriff's sale [Dinkelspiel 67]) The Farmers and Merchants Bank was able to make loans at one to one-and-a-half to two percent a month, the same rate offered by banks in San Francisco.

As new settlers streamed into the region, many of them veterans of the Civil War, they could turn to the Farmers and Merchants Bank for funds to buy farms and plant crops. The 1870s were a time of experimentation in Los Angeles, when men and merchants were still trying to figure out the crops and businesses that would flourish in the region. Just a few years earlier, California and its temperate climate seemed an ideal place to raise silkworms ("Mulberry Trees and Cuttings"). Aspiring farmers planted thousands of mulberry trees and imported silkworms from China, in part to capture subsidies offered by the state Legislature. The fad faded as quickly as it started ("Silk Culture in California"; "Silk Culture"). Farmers then turned their attention to growing wheat, barley, walnuts, and Mission grapes, which were used to make wine. A number of growers tried raising oranges, and the number of fruit and nut trees planted in the region tripled in just a few years. One inventive farmer even managed to raise pineapples (*History of Los Angeles County* 60–66).

Two brothers, Otto J. and Oswald F. Zahn, capitalized on the growing travel between Los Angeles and Catalina Island, located twenty-two miles offshore. The construction of a railroad in 1869 from Los Angeles to San Pedro made getting to Catalina Island much easier and hearty adventurers would camp out and swim in the blue waters. But once on the island, they were cut off. The Zahns filled a void with the Catalina Pigeon Messengers, a flock of homing pigeons that carried news between the island and the towns on the mainland. It was cause for celebration when the Zahns' prized pigeon, Blue Jim, flew the channel in only fifty minutes (Newmark 430).

As the region prospered, Hellman made his own business investments, and he soon saw his fortune grow. He invested heavily in city utilities[8] and was soon a major stockholder in the privately-run gas and water companies.[9] He invested in one of the city's first trolley lines[10] and by the mid-1880s was Los Angeles' dominant trolley magnate.[11] He also helped form some other banks, most notably the Security Savings Bank and Trust Company and the Los Angeles Savings Bank ("Loan and Trust" 2; Dinkelspiel 117).[12]

Land formed the basis for much of Hellman's fortune.[13] He bought his first parcel in 1863 and kept buying steadily until he became one of the region's largest landholders and the city's largest taxpayer. (The *Los Angeles Express* reported on Dec. 29, 1886 that Isaias paid the most taxes of any man in Los Angeles—more than $14,000.) He built business blocks around the city, including one on the site of his original dry goods store. Hellman bought large chunks of Rancho San Pedro in the 1860s (Isaias W. Hellman vs. Henry N. Alexander, case no. 1895). In 1871, the Farmers and Merchants Bank foreclosed on the 13,000 acre Rancho Cucamonga in what his now San Bernardino County. The bank sold a third of the property to a San Francisco syndicate, and Hellman, John Downey, and his cousin Isaiah M. Hellman bought the bulk of the rancho. They spun off another third to develop, and planted wheat, wine, barley and raisins on the rest. Over the next decade, Hellman would acquire a third-interest in the vast Rancho Alamitos near Long Beach, and a portion of the Repetto Ranch south of Alhambra, among other lands. He also owned much of the area known as Boyle Heights (Dinkelspiel 50).

Hellman most actively invested in land with Downey and the pioneer horticulturist Ozro Childs. In 1876, the trio had bought thousands of acres in the southwest section of Los Angeles, in an area covered with grassy fields and little else. Intending to subdivide the land, they took out an ad that ran an entire column length in the Sept. 17, 1877 edition of *Los Angeles Herald*, dwarfing other real estate notices:

> Lots for sale! Offers the best opportunity for delightful homesteads of any that has ever been offered for sale to the public. The whole tract is level. The soil is excellent. This is really the West end of our beautiful city, with the benefit of FRESH, PURE BREEZES FROM THE OCEAN, uncontaminated by gas or sewer effluvia.

Despite the hyperbole, the land was not easy to sell, as it was about three miles from the Plaza, then the center of Los Angeles. There was a trolley line (started by the partners) running through the property, and Agricultural Park, the racetrack, was nearby, but the $300 parcels were not selling briskly. Part of the problem was oversupply; by the late 1870s there was a miniature boom in the region. Almost every businessman in Los Angeles, it seemed, was in the real estate business.

When Robert Widney announced in May 1879 that the Methodists were looking for land on which to put a new university, Hellman and his partners jumped. They knew that having a school nearby would make West Los Angeles an attractive place to settle, and that it would spawn new houses and farms. Other large landowners felt similarly and soon Widney had multiple offers of land (Lifton and Moore 5).

To make their offer more attractive, Isaias, Downey, and Childs proposed to extend their trolley line, the Main Street and Agricultural Park Railway, directly onto the new campus. That enticement may have made the difference because in July 1879 Widney accepted their offer of 308 lots of land, about 110 acres (Map of West Los Angeles). The bulk would be sold off to form an endowment for the new university, named the "University of Southern California," and the rest would be used for the school. The donation instantly catapulted Hellman, Downey and Childs into the group of men regarded as founders of the university, a position recognized to this day (*Los Angeles Herald* Sept. 5, 1880). Hellman's contribution to USC captured the attention of California Governor George Perkins, who appointed Hellman to the Board of Regents of the University of California in 1881. Hellman would sit as a Regent for thirty-seven years, serving much of that time on the board's powerful finance committee.

As president of the Farmers and Merchants Bank, Hellman was in a perfect position to learn about business deals. While the bank mostly carried mortgages, in the 1880s it directed an increasing amount of money into promising industries. Before lending funds, Isaias tried to determine whether a business would help the region's economy grow. If it could, he was more inclined to fund it, for he thought the positive effects of the loan would have a ripple effect. If he thought the proposal didn't have a chance, he would turn it down. For example, when Henry Wilshire asked the Farmers and Merchants Bank in November 1895 for a loan to buy thirty-five acres for his eponymous boulevard, the bank refused him (Wilshire, Letter to Farmers and Merchants Bank).

Hellman also put money into a few risky ventures—but only when he decided that the men behind the enterprise were trustworthy. In the mid-1880s, Los Angeles, like much of America, was oil crazy. America had been obsessed by oil since 1859, when Colonel Edwin Drake discovered rock oil while drilling a well in Titusville, Pennsylvania. The automobile had not been invented yet, but an increasingly industrialized America still needed oil for lamps and heating, and its byproduct, gas, for illumination.

Residents of the Los Angeles region had been using oil products from the time of the earliest settlers. The region was dotted with "brea," a sticky tar-like substance that Native Americans had used to waterproof baskets and Californios had used to tar their roofs. In 1855, Andres Pico started to excavate the asphalt that lay in pools of oil on his large Rancho San Fernando. His discovery promoted other businessmen to start exploring, and within a few years there was a mini-oil boom. Hellman's partner, Downey, Phineas Banning, and B. D. Wilson founded the Pioneer Oil Co., one of the earliest companies formed to explore for oil. Despite spending hundreds of thousands of dollars to drill wells, the Pioneer Oil Company never found a rich strike and went out of business.

By 1887, there were only four companies exploring for oil in southern California ("Oil and Gas Yielding Formations of California"). One was the Hardison & Stewart Oil Company, founded in 1883 by Lyman Stewart and Wallace Hardison, who had worked together successfully in Pennsylvania. They had moved their operations to Los Angeles and spent four years traipsing around the region, digging hole after hole in a fruitless search for oil. They borrowed all they could and soon found themselves broke and $183,000 in debt, with no oil in sight.

The men went to see Hellman. "We didn't know what to do or where to turn," said Stewart. "We owed IWH all that we dared to owe him. But we saw him and told him that the Hardison & Stewart Co. needed $20,000. Mr. Hellman was in ill health and was preparing for a six-month trip abroad. He was calling in all loans. I told him how we were situated and how badly we needed the money. He replied, 'There are millionaires in this town that I won't lend another dollar to because they are doing nothing to benefit the community, but you are doing something to develop the resources of the county. Let me see your statement'. That made us tremble. We were then at the high water mark of our liabilities and our statement showed we owed one hundred and eighty-three thousand dollars. Mr. Hellman looked at the statement and said, 'Draw your checks for ten thousand more, and I will order them paid'. He did not ask for any collateral" (*Pacific Petroleum Record*).

The men discovered oil. Their company was eventually known as Unocal.

*****

Hellman's history repeated itself in 1893 with Edward Doheney and Charles Canfield. The two men were veteran miners and explorers when they first met in New Mexico. Canfield moved to Los Angeles in the mid-1880s and made and lost a fortune, buying and selling real estate during the boom. Doheny had followed his friend to Los Angeles in hopes of getting rich but soon found himself living in a rundown boarding house on Sixth and Figueroa Streets with his wife and sickly seven-year old daughter, out of funds and out of ideas. Then one day he noticed a wagon rolling past his hotel, its back heaped with black pitch. Doheny asked the driver what it was and where it came from and soon was rushing towards Westlake Park. He found a hole oozing with a tarry substance. He picked it up. He smelled it and noticed it had a sweet odor. He asked a nearby worker what the brea could be used for, and learned that it could be burned for fuel (Davis).

Doheny had been a miner and prospector for twenty years at that point, and he realized there might be a business in collecting and selling the brea. Los Angeles was fueled by coal, which was expensive at twenty dollars a ton. Doheny thought there might be a market for a lower-priced heating and light source.

But where would Doheny get the money to acquire land? Canfield was broke, his last fortune having evaporated in a downturn in the real estate market. Nonetheless, Doheny managed to convince him to set up a partnership. Canfield went to see Hellman and asked to borrow $500. He had no money, no prospects, just the idea that there must be reserves of oil lurking below the city. No bank would lend to him, but Hellman saw something he liked in Canfield, a determination that would not quit. Isaias lent Canfield the money. A short time later, using a drill attached to a makeshift, twenty-foot tall derrick constructed out of four by fours, Doheny and Canfield penetrated a hard outcropping of rock two hundred feet into the ground. When the metal bit broke through the strata, it uncovered a pool of dark, viscous oil, the biggest strike ever uncovered in Los Angeles.

With Hellman's help, the men created one of one of the state's largest and most lucrative oil companies (Hellman, Letter to Whitney).

*****

By late 1889, Hellman was starting to feel restless in Los Angeles. The boom that swept the region from 1886 to 1888 had brought huge profits to the region, funds that made their way into the Farmers and Merchants bank and the other financial institutions with which Isaias was associated. After living in southern California for thirty years, Hellman itched to expand, to become a bigger player in the world of finance.

In 1890, Hellman left Los Angeles to take over the presidency of the Nevada Bank in San Francisco, a city that had 300,000 residents compared to Los Angeles' 50,000. The Nevada Bank had been founded in 1875 by the four "Silver Kings," John Mackay, James Flood, James Fair and William O'Brien and had at one time been capitalized at ten million dollars, the most of any financial institution in the country. But the bank had fallen on hard times after its cashier had tried unsuccessfully to corner the wheat market in 1887.

In 1890, Hellman raised $2.5 million in capital to take control of the bank. So many men clamored to buy the stock that he had to turn some away, an indication of Hellman's growing reputation. "Millionaires stood in rows for hours waiting their chance to subscribe to the stock and men feeble from age were represented among them," the *Los Angeles Herald* reported in 1890. "One of the best known businessmen, not only of San Francisco, but of the state, told the writer that he was recently present at a discussion concerning Mr. Hellman's financial status in which he was held up as the wealthiest Hebrew in America with the total being placed at $40,000,000. One thing is certain, however, and that is that his brief connection with the Nevada Bank has been signalized by the most remarkable occurrence ever noted in the financial annals of California" (Undated newspaper article).

The new shareholders of the Nevada Bank were some of the most influential men in the country, including Meyer Lehman, Hellman's brother-in-law and the head of Lehman Brothers in New York; Levi Strauss, the head of the clothing concern; and Antoine Borel, a Swiss banker and bond dealer. Hellman did not neglect his friends from Los Angeles. He sold stock to William Germain, the Los Angeles fruit grower, William Perry, the lumberman who now ran the Los Angeles City Water Company, and Abraham Haas, a partner with Herman Hellman in Hellman, Haas, and Co. Abraham Haas's brother William, who ran Haas Brothers in San Francisco, also got shares. (The Hellmans and the Haases came from the same town in Germany and had grown up together.) Isaac Van Nuys and John Wolfskill also purchased stakes in the bank.

While many of the investors were Jewish, Hellman was careful to create a diverse board of directors. "I have selected an excellent board of directors all strong men, privately speaking seven Christians and including myself four Jews," Hellman wrote to his brother-in-law in England. "I have done this to avoid the idea which exists with other banks here of making a Jewish bank or Catholic or any other institution. I want it to be a popular institution—I think it is so considered, if not I will endeavor my best to make it so" (Hellman, Letter to Newgass).

The news that Hellman was leaving Los Angeles to take over a San Francisco bank filled the pages of the papers around the state. Editors in Los Angeles wrote pieces questioning how Isaias' move would impact the city. They soon suggested it would expand the flow of capital between the two cities. "No deleterious effect can come to Los Angeles from the proposed change," said an editorial in the February 24, 1890 edition of the *Los Angeles Herald*. "Mr. Hellman, whose interests here are immense, will be at the head of a bank that will be from the moment he enters it the controlling influence on the finances of the Coast. It will be his pleasure and his interest both to aid in every legitimate enterprise thought of in Los Angeles. He will have control of unlimited funds, and if any industry can show him it is one of merit, it may safely count on his encouragement."

Moving to San Francisco let Hellman expand into new financial markets. Hellman became friends with Collis Huntington, one of the founders of the Southern Pacific Railroad. Huntington apparently enjoyed discussing business matters with Isaias. He told John Mackay that Isaias was "one of the ablest bankers" he knew. When Huntington came to San Francisco, he made a point of talking to Isaias. "I have been coming to see you almost every day since I came out, but everyday seems to bring business that holds me very closely to the corner of Fourth and Townsend Streets; not that I have any special business, only I wanted to come in and talk matters over generally with you," Huntington wrote Isaias (Huntington, Letter to Hellman).

Hellman and Huntington had first met in 1876 when Isaias was part of a group of businessmen lobbying to bring the Southern Pacific to Los Angeles. In the ensuing decades, the power of Southern Pacific had grown enormously, as it expanded its routes and control of freight rates throughout the state. Its political arm extended into numerous political campaigns and a growing chorus of critics had started to denounce the influence of the Southern Pacific.

The Southern Pacific was one of the Nevada Bank's biggest customers, and Hellman soon began to make a market for the rail line's bonds. During the early 1890s, he sold from ten to fifteen million dollars of the railroad's bonds (Hellman, Letter to Speyer), as well as another ten million dollars in bonds for an SP subsidiary, the Market Street Railway (*San Francisco Call*).

The issue of expanding the port of Los Angeles tested Hellman's ability to juggle his loyalties between northern and southern California and not offend any of his friends. The waters off the coast of San Pedro had never been deep enough to permit ocean-going vessels to dock near the shore, and Los Angeles' business community looked to the federal government to build a massive breakwater. After two federal committees recommended that San Pedro be developed, Huntington threw a monkey-wrench into the process by proclaiming that Santa Monica would be the better port and should get the federal appropriation.[14] By 1894, Southern Pacific had constructed a 4,300-foot wharf extending into the ocean at Santa Monica, and Huntington wanted to capitalize on his one million dollar investment.

The battle over the port would rage for years, pitting Huntington against a determined group of businessmen from Los Angeles, including the Chamber of Commerce and Harrison Gray Otis, who turned the pages of his *Los Angeles Times* into a forum for the Free Harbor Association. The businessmen favored San Pedro over Santa Monica because it was the city's traditional port. They also feared that Southern Pacific was too firmly entrenched in Santa Monica and would use its position to jack up shipping rates. They did not want "Uncle Collis," as the newspapers called him, to become even more dominant ("The Harbor Question").

Isaias tried to tread a middle ground by endorsing the development of both ports, thereby not antagonizing either Huntington or Otis. It was relatively easy to maintain neutrality since he now lived in San Francisco. "If possible, why not have appropriations for both harbors?" Isaias wrote to Otis (Hellman, Letter to Otis). After Congress finally concluded that San Pedro was superior to Santa Monica, the Farmers and Merchants Bank lent $50,000 to help build a breakwater (Cleland 66).

It was around 1894 that Hellman became acquainted with another Huntington, one who would ultimately play a large role in Isaias' business life and have a profound impact on the development of Southern California. That man was Huntington's nephew, Henry Edwards, who had come to San Francisco in 1892 to represent his family's interests in the Southern Pacific. One of his early tasks was to secure rights of way for expansion, and he and Hellman met during negotiations over property near Pasadena. The two men later worked together to raise funds for the modernization of San Francisco's trolley lines. Hellman's Nevada Bank handled a ten million dollar bond issue to electrify some of the lines and modernize the tracks.

Even while in San Francisco, Hellman had maintained his interest in the Los Angeles trolley systems. He had actively developed trolley lines until the mid-1880s, and was a major investor in the City Railroad, the Los Angeles Cable Railway, and the Los Angeles and Pacific Railway Company. He also held a large number of bonds for the Temple Street Cable Railway.

While working together, Hellman and Huntington began to talk about the advantages of consolidating and modernizing the trolleys in Los Angeles, much as Huntington had done for the rail lines in San Francisco. There were more than a half-dozen companies operating the various lines in the region, creating a mish-mash of technologies and routes.

Los Angeles residents who had watched a myriad of men and companies try and tame the city's transportation business learned of yet another attempt when they plunked down their three cents for the September 14, 1898 edition of the *Los Angeles Times*. When they opened the paper to local news on page four, their eyes were drawn to an extra large article outlined in black. "Gobbled by the S. P." the headline read in breathless type. "Huntington & Co. Take in the Los Angeles Railway."

The details were sketchy, as the article was only a few paragraphs long. But the gist suggested that the Southern Pacific Railroad had purchased the bulk of the rail lines in Los Angeles. The Huntington family, led by Collis and his nephew Henry, had been quietly negotiating throughout the summer for the trolley company that ran cars throughout the downtown business district, the article read.

Throughout the day, reporters from the *Times* and other newspapers raced around town trying to collect more information. When word got out that Isaias might have something to do with the purchase, reporters rushed to the Farmers and Merchants Bank to interview his brother Herman Hellman. "That is a matter on which I cannot give definite information," Herman told the papers. "Although I am interested with my brother, Isaias W. Hellman, in the banking business, he is the one who is interested in the Los Angeles Railway system" ("The Railway Deal").

Details soon emerged and it turned out that the *Los Angeles Times* had gotten some important facts right—and some other critical facts wrong. Henry Huntington, his Uncle Collis, and his son Howard had made an offer for five of Los Angeles' six rail lines. The buyers paid $3.9 million for the companies and planned to issue five million dollars in bonds to pay off the debt and make improvements. But the Huntingtons were not the only buyers. Hellman and a syndicate including San Francisco bankers Antoine Borel and Christian de Guigne had purchased a forty-five percent interest in the deal. This was a private transaction, not one masterminded by Southern Pacific.

Still, the fact that there were three Huntingtons involved was great fodder for the newspapers as Collis Huntington and his strong-arm tactics were widely feared. On Friday, September 16, the *Times* ran a large cartoon on its front page picturing a sweating, bearded Collis Huntington holding the entire earth in his arms, with a Los Angeles Street Railway trolley car gripped in one hand. The cartoon had a label "The Earth. This Property is Owned by the Southern Pacific Railway." In the cartoon, Huntington is thinking to himself: "I wonder if there is anything else I have forgotten?"

The 1898 creation of the LARY, or the Los Angeles Railway, ushered in an era of close cooperation between Hellman and Henry Huntington, one that would lead to some of the most important developments the Los Angeles basin had ever seen.[15] Hellman's Nevada Bank and Union Trust Company would issue a series of bonds that would not only fund LARY, but the famed Pacific Electric, whose red trolley cars would one day extend hundreds of miles in the region. To get electricity for the electric cars, Hellman and his syndicate also bought $500,000 in debt from the San Gabriel Electric Power Company. A few years later Huntington and Hellman joined with William Kerckhoff to start Pacific Light and Power Company, which brought electricity from the Kern River to Los Angeles on more than one hundred miles of electric wire ("Huntington's New Venture"). Hellman's Union Trust Company of San Francisco floated ten million dollars in bonds to pay for the construction ("Bonded Debt Made for Ten Millions"). That company was later folded into Southern California Edison.[16]

Hellman did not just provide capital to the enterprise. In the early years of the partnership, before Huntington made Los Angeles his home, Hellman knew the area better than the railroad man. Three years after the Huntington-Hellman syndicate created LARY, Hellman pushed for a more expansive rail line, one that would link cities to one another, not just deliver passengers to various points within city limits.

"I have spent a month in Los Angeles and found that city very much improved," Isaias wrote Huntington in May 1901. "I think the time is on hand when we should commence building suburban roads out of the city. If we do not do so soon, others will. There is a great deal of idle capital and men with energy and brains waiting for good business openings in Los Angeles" (Hellman, Letter to Huntington). Isaias had even gone as far as asking W. H. Holabird, a LARY employee, to look at a map and sketch out possible rail routes to Long Beach, San Pedro, Redondo and elsewhere (Holabird, Letter to Huntington).

"As for building suburban roads out of Los Angeles, I agree with you that the time has come when we should begin doing it," Huntington responded a week later (Huntington, Letter to Hellman).

In November, 1901, the men started the Pacific Electric.

Huntington gets much of the credit for creating his extensive transportation network, which many people believe contributed to Los Angeles' urban sprawl. Hellman, however, was key in making Huntington see the possibilities of the southern part of the state and finding the capital to facilitate growth. Hellman provided the vision and money during a critical period, just has he had with Otis, Stewart and Hardison, Doheny and Canfield, and with many others.

Hellman went on to take the lead in many more endeavors, including construction of significant buildings in Los Angeles' downtown;[17] a leadership role in the sale of bonds for the Russo-Japanese War (Dinkelspiel 307) and Liberty Bonds in World War I (Wells Fargo Nevada National Bank Minute Book); the development of property throughout the region, and more. At the height of his power in the early part of the twentieth century, after he had merged the Nevada Bank with Wells Fargo Bank,[18] he commanded more than one hundred million dollars in capital, funds that were put to use to improve California's infrastructure (Dinkelspiel 289).

When Hellman died on April 9, 1920 after a brief bout of pneumonia, he was seventy-seven. The news of his death was bannered across the tops of newspapers. Flags were lowered to half-staff at various banks.

"In the regrettable death of Mr. Hellman, this community and the entire Pacific Coast suffers an irreparable loss," Herbert Fleishhacker, the president of the Anglo London and Paris National Bank told the *San Francisco Chronicle*. "A pioneer of Western financiers, his virile energy, sterling ability and high sense of honor were combined to wield a potent influence upon the development of the West, to make him an outstanding international figure. His public interests were as wide as his modestly unheralded private philanthropies were generous" (*San Francisco Chronicle*).

Traces of Hellman still can be seen throughout the state. There are Hellman Streets in Los Angeles, Long Beach, Alhambra, Rosemead, Rancho Cucamonga, and Oakland. A fund bearing his name at the University of California at Berkeley has awarded more than four million dollars in scholarships ("The Isaias W. Hellman Scholarship Fund"). He was lauded as a founder at the University of Southern California's 125th anniversary celebration.[19] His old home in Lake Tahoe is now Sugar Pine Point State Park.

Even after his death, Hellman's estate continued to build the state's economy. On June 23, 1921, the Shell Oil Company, drilling on land on Signal Hill owned jointly by the Hellman and Bixby families, struck a huge reservoir of oil. The well, named Alamitos #1, was the largest source of oil ever discovered in California and the discovery reignited the oil rush. Oil was discovered on another parcel of Hellman's land in Seal Beach, on land that was part of Rancho Alamitos. It is still producing oil in 2009. It is one of the oldest family-operated oil operations in the state.[20]

There is no question that Isaias Hellman played a major role in the economic development of California, one equal with the financial titans with whom he routinely did business in the latter half of the nineteenth and beginning of the twentieth centuries. That era is filled with many well-known rags-to-riches stories, such as the rise of the Carnegies and Rockefellers of the Northeast and the Astors of the Northwest. What is notable, however, is that Hellman was regarded primarily as a master builder and community leader and only secondarily as a Jew. Other Jews, such as the Seligmans, Lehmans, Guggenheims, and others in New York City, rose to prominence but were always categorized by their religion. By settling in Southern California, an undeveloped outpost sufficiently far out on the cultural frontier, Hellman was able to escape those constraints. In that rough and tumble world, a self-made man who also happened to be Jewish could achieve great things and could mix and move in the highest societal circles. Southern California, unlike other regions, had sufficient social fluidity that a Jewish individual could rise to be admired as a mover and shaper of the California West.

Notes

1. The 1880 census put the population at just over 11,183 and the 1890 census put the number at 50,395. Historian Robert Fogelson (21) estimates the population at 20,000 in 1885.
2. Besides being president of Wells Fargo Bank and the Farmers and Merchants Bank, during his lifetime Hellman served as president of the Nevada Bank, the Union Trust Company, the Southern Trust Company, the United States National Bank, the Pasadena National Bank and the First National Bank of Monrovia. He also served as a director of the Security Savings Bank, the Los Angeles Savings Bank, the Main Street Savings Bank, the Southern Trust Company, the National Bank of Long Beach, the Long Beach Savings Bank, the Fidelity Trust Company of Tacoma, Washington, the Farmers and Merchants Bank of Redondo Beach, Banca Italia, and Colombus Savings and Loan.
3. Hellmans had been in Los Angeles as least as early as 1854, when Hellman's cousins Isaiah M, Samuel M, and Herman M. Hellman arrived. Hellman's maternal uncle, Israel Fleishman, opened a hardware store in Los Angeles with Julius Sichel, who may have been a relative of Philip Sichel.
4. Abraham Edelman was hired as the rabbi for Congregation B'Nai B'rith in 1862. From the start, Edelman and his congregation adapted Judaism to fit the American frontier. B'nai B'rith had a Sunday school for children, a mixed choir, an organ, and sermons and prayers in English as well as Hebrew. For a fuller discussion see Stern and Kramer.
5. Bank deposit slip, private collection of Katherine Hellman Black, great-granddaughter of I. W. Hellman.
6. There is no information available that determines when Hellman actually set up formal banking services. He opened his store in 1865 and sold it in 1868, so the date lies in those years. This was before John Downey opened his bank, which is why some historians have called Hellman the first banker of Los Angeles.
7. For a more complete discussion of Workman and Temple, see Dinkelspiel 46–48.
8. Hellman sat on the board of the gas company and the San Pedro Railroad; see Dinkelspiel 189.
9. By 1901 Hellman was the largest shareholder of the City Water Company, with 1,200 shares. See letter from William H. Perry to I. W. Hellman.
10. In 1874, Hellman, John Downey, William Workman and F. P. F. Temple invested funds to start the Main Street and Agricultural Park Railway, which traveled from the Plaza down Main Street to Agricultural Park (Dinkelspiel 101).
11. Hellman was involved with the creation or financing of numerous trolley systems in Los Angeles. In 1883, he, William Brodrick and John Wheeler, created the City Railroad of Los Angeles. They merged it in 1886 with the Central Railroad (Dinkelspiel 116). Hellman was also a bond holder in the Temple Street Railway and an investor in the Los Angeles Cable Railway, among others.

12. In 1956, the Security Trust and Savings Bank, then known as Security Pacific, absorbed the Farmers and Merchants Bank. That entity was later bought by Bank of America.
13. Hellman bought 8,000 acres of the former Rancho Cucamonga in San Bernardino County in 1871; acquired a third ownership of 26,000 acres of Rancho Alamitos in 1881, and owned 800 acres of Rancho San Pedro, as well as large interests in the Repetto Ranch and Rancho San Gertrudes. He also bought numerous lots throughout downtown Los Angeles.
14. For a good description of this battle, see Quiett.
15. LARY was created by the purchase of the Los Angeles Consolidated Railway, the Main Street and Agricultural Park Railway, the Main and Fifth Street Railway, the Main, Fifth, and San Pedro Street Railway, and the Los Angeles Railway. The new system initially had 168 miles of track. By December 1898, two other acquisitions had increased the rail line's system to two hundred miles of track. See Dinkelspiel 188. In addition to building rail lines, the friendship between Hellman and Huntington led to the latter's purchase of what is today the Huntington Library and Gardens. Hellman's Farmers and Merchants Bank had foreclosed on the property and in January 1903, sold it to Huntington and Hellman's San Francisco syndicate, which retained a thirty-nine percent interest in the property. See Agreement between H. E. Huntington and Antoine Borel.
16. Southern California Edison bought Pacific Light and Power in 1917.
17. Hellman had started constructing buildings downtown in the 1870s, including a three story brick building he put up with Ozro Childs on the east side of North Main Street in 1875. In 1905, Hellman built a new headquarters for his Farmers and Merchants Bank on the site of his old homestead on the corner of 4th and Main in Los Angeles, as well as a large L-shaped office building. Hellman also constructed what is now known as the Hellman-Quan building on the Plaza.
18. When Edward Harriman acquired a controlling interest in Southern Pacific in 1901, he also gained control of Wells Fargo Bank. Harriman was more interested in the cash-producing Wells Fargo Express than the underperforming bank unit and he asked Hellman to take it off his hands. Hellman merged his Nevada National Bank with Wells Fargo Bank in early 1905 to form the Wells Fargo Nevada National Bank with fifteen million dollars in deposits.
19. The author was invited by USC to give an address about Hellman and his role in the founding of the university in September 2005. More than 350 people attended the talk, including USC President Steven Sample. The event was sponsored by the Casden Institute for the Study of the Jewish Role in American Life, and the Huntington-USC Institute on California and the West.
20. The Bixby family owned and operated oil lands in the Seal Beach/Long Beach area until 2007.

Works Cited

Agreement between H. E. Huntington and Antoine Borel. June 1903. Henry Huntington Papers. San Marino, CA: Huntington Library.

"The Bar Mitzvah of a Banker's Son, Los Angeles 1884." *Western States Jewish Historical Quarterly* 5.3 (April 1973).

Benjamin, I. J. *Three Years in America, 1859–1862*. Vol. 1. Philadelphia: Jewish Publication Society, 1956.

"Bonded Debt Made for Ten Millions." *Los Angeles Times* Aug. 24, 1902.

Cleland, Robert Glass and Putnam, Frank B. *Isaias W. Hellman and the Farmers and Merchants Bank*. San Marino, CA: Huntington Library, 1965.

Cross, Ira. *Financing an Empire: History of Banking in California*. Chicago and San Francisco: Clarke, 1927.

Davis, Margaret Leslie. *Dark Side of Fortune: Triumph and Scandal in the Life of Oil Tycoon Edward L. Doheny*. Berkeley: Univ. of California, 1998.

Dinkelspiel, Frances. *Towers of Gold: How One Jewish Immigrant Named Isaias Hellman Created California*. New York: St. Martin's, 2008.

"Dry Goods." *Los Angeles News* April 15, 1865.

"Dry Goods & Clothing Emporium." *Los Angeles Semi-Weekly News* July 6, 1866.

Engh, Michael E. "Charity Knows Neither Race Nor Creed: Jewish Philanthropy to Roman Catholic Projects in Los Angeles, 1856–1876." *Western States Jewish Historical Quarterly* 21.2 (1989).

Fogelson, Robert. *The Fragmented Metropolis*. Berkeley: Univ. of California, 1993.

"The Harbor Question." *Los Angeles Times* March 14, 1894: 6.

"Hebrew Synagogue." *Los Angeles Star* Aug. 24, 1872.

Hellman, Isaias W. Letter to Henry Huntington. May 21, 1901. MS 981 Box 35, vol. 27. San Francisco: California Historical Society.

———. Letter to Benjamin Newgass. March 28, 1890. MS 981 Box 29, letter book 8. San Francisco: California Historical Society.

———. Letter Harrison Gray Otis. Oct 12, 1894. MS 981 Box 32, vol. 17. San Francisco: California Historical Society.

———. Letter to James Speyer. Sept. 22, 1900. MS 981, vol. 26, 399. San Francisco: California Historical Society.

———. Letter to Casper Whitney. Sept. 30, 1919. MS 981 Box 24, vol. 51. San Francisco: California Historical Society.

History of Los Angeles County. Oakland, CA.: Thompson and West, 1880.

Holabird, W. H. Letter to Henry Huntington. May 3, 1901. MS 981, Box 8. San Francisco: California Historical Society.

"Huntington's New Venture." *Los Angeles Times* March 26, 1902.

Huntington, Collis. Letter to Isaias W. Hellman. March 7, 1894. MS 981 Box 4. San Francisco: California Historical Society.

Huntington, Henry. Letter to Isaias W. Hellman. May 27, 1901. MS 981, Box 8. San Francisco: California Historical Society.

"The Isaias W. Hellman Scholarship Fund." The Annual Report of Berkeley's Endowment, 2007–08. Berkeley: Univ. of California, Berkeley.

Isaias W. Hellman vs. Henry N. Alexander. Case no. 1895, Los Angeles County Court Records. San Marino, CA: Huntington Library.

Ledger, 1865. Hellman Family Papers, 1850–1971. Box 24, folder 26. Wells Fargo Bank Archives.

Lifton, Sarah, and Moore, Annette. *The University of Southern California: 1880 to 2005*. Los Angeles: Figueroa, 2007.

"Loan and Trust." *Los Angeles Times* June 2, 1888: 2.

Los Angeles Daily Republican. Dec. 4, 1876: 2.

Los Angeles Express. Dec. 29, 1886.

Los Angeles Herald. Sept. 5, 1880.

Los Angeles Star. Sept. 13, 1877.

Map of West Los Angeles, Shaded Lots Donated for an Endowment Fund. 1880. MS 981. San Francisco: California Historical Society.

Mesmer, Joseph. "Some of My Los Angeles Jewish Neighbors." *Western States Jewish Historical Quarterly*, 3.3 (April 1975).

"Mulberry Trees and Cuttings." *Los Angeles Semi-Weekly News* March 26, 1869.

"New Banking Enterprise." *Los Angeles News*. Sept. 1, 1868.

Newmark, Harris. *Sixty Years in Southern California*. Cambridge, MA: Riverside, 1930.

"Oil and Gas Yielding Formations of California." *California State Mining Bureau Bulletin* 19 (Nov. 9, 1900).

Otis, Harrison Gray. Letter to Isaias W. Hellman. April 25, 1894. Isaias W. Hellman Papers, 1865–1929, MS 981. San Francisco: California Historical Society.

Quiett, Glenn Chesney. "The Fight for a Free Port." *Los Angeles, Biography of a City*. Ed. John and LaRee Caughey. Berkeley: Univ. of California, 1977.

Pacific Petroleum Record. Feb. 1919.

Perry, William H. Letter to I. W. Hellman. Nov. 1898. MS 981. San Francisco: California Historical Society.

"The Railway Deal," Los Angeles *Times*, Sept. 15, 1898.

San Francisco Call. Oct. 21, 1895.

San Francisco Chronicle. April 10, 1920: 1.

"Silk Culture." *Los Angeles Star* June 12, 1868.

"Silk-Culture in California." *Overland Monthly* 4 (1870): 452–57.

Stern, Norton B., and Kramer, William M. "Jewish Padre to the Pueblo: Pioneer Los Angeles Rabbi Abraham Wolf Edelman." *Western States Jewish Historical Quarterly* 3.4 (July 1971).

Undated newspaper article. MS 981, Box 1, folder 6. San Francisco: California Historical Society.

Vorspan, Max, and Gartner, Lloyd P. *History of the Jews of Los Angeles*. San Marino, CA: Huntington Library, 1970.

Wells Fargo Nevada National Bank Minute Book, June 26, 1917. Aug. 1911–Jan. 1924. Wells Fargo Bank Archives.

Wilshire, Henry. Letter to Farmers and Merchants Bank. Nov. 13, 1885. Hellman Family Papers, Box 6, folder 11. Wells Fargo Bank Archives.

A Twice-Told Journey: Sarah Newmark in the Russian Polish Shtetl—How a Jewish California Matron Confronted Her European Heritage

Karen S. Wilson[1]

INTRODUCTION

In 1887, Sarah Newmark, a wealthy matron of a German-Jewish family from Los Angeles, along with other members of her family, visited Grajewo, a small village inside the Russian Pale of Settlement. We know a good deal about this visit because Newmark wrote about it—twice, one contemporaneous with the visit in time and place, and the other removed from it by three years and several thousand miles.[2] Why did she travel to a shtetl while on a European grand tour?[3] Neither version gives an explicit answer to that question. However, a comparison of the two versions points to a motive shaped by family history and contemporary circumstances at home and abroad. Further, the differences between the versions suggest that, during the intervening time, Newmark engaged in a rethinking and reordering of her intertwined identities of Jewish, American, and upper middle class. The revision of journey and identity took place in Los Angeles at a time when, increasingly, class, religion, and race defined the social order—especially in the American Southwest.

Newmark's contemporaneous travel diary reveals anxieties about being a Jew in a modern society, while the journal she wrote later offers a response to those anxieties. When Newmark first wrote about visiting Grajewo, she preserved an emotional and even a somewhat disturbing encounter with co-religionists. When she revised that account back home in Los Angeles, she produced a story of "novel sights," American privilege, and acculturated sensibilities. At first glance, the different emphasis in the second version appears to be simply reflective of her elite position in LA society. I would like to suggest, however, that Newmark refashioned her narrative deliberately, if unconsciously, to obscure any association, past, present and future, between the Russian Jews and the American Newmarks. Read in comparison with the original and in context of a changing Los Angeles, the revised version provides a useful cultural object lesson by showing how she attempted to remove herself from troublesome associations of ethno-religious identity and recast herself instead in what she perceived to be more socially beneficial identities. Dedicating the journal explicitly to her children, Newmark used her Grajewo visit to teach them, in her terms, how best to handle one's Jewish identity in "modern" America and particularly in Southern California just before the start of the twentieth century. A closer look at those elements that come to the surface in the private reflections of an elite Jewish Angeleno can serve to highlight aspects of social integration as a contingent, on-going process, rather than an achieved condition, for Jews in the multicultural American West.

In examining the history of Los Angeles Jewry, Newmark's personal reflections provide an intimate complement to her husband's memoir, *Sixty Years in Southern California*, written nearly thirty years later and still used as a primary source for nineteenth-century LA (Harris Newmark). Mrs. Newmark's accounts of life, new sights, and customs far away from home—while still ensconced in the comfort of family and engaged in the routine of responsibilities—offer an expansive and extended encounter with a self-aware, American-born, Jewish daughter of immigrants from the Southwest. In these narratives, one therefore gains a rare opportunity to understand the meanings of those identities and their interplay at the end of the nineteenth century. Even more unusual, the existence of both a "first draft" and a later revision frames a moment of social transition that well illustrates the social dynamic of Newmark's world.

SARAH NEWMARK, HER FAMILY AND THEIR LOS ANGELES

Forty-six years old when she traveled to Europe for the first time, Sarah Newmark had been born in New York City, the third of six children of Rosa Levy from London, England, and Joseph Newmark from Neumark, West Prussia. Her father had arrived in the US in 1824, as a widower. He married his second wife, Rosa, in 1835. With a growing family in tow, Joseph and Rosa lived in St. Louis, Dubuque, Iowa, and San Francisco before arriving in Los

Angeles in 1854. The journey to the West apparently was motivated mainly by the lure of frontier opportunities but included at least one return east (Harris Newmark 122).

Like her siblings, Newmark was educated at home and in public schools. She finished her formal education in Schoolhouse Number One, the first public school constructed in Los Angeles. Her older brother, Myer, tutored her in Hebrew, while she was examined in French by her mother. She showed some literacy in Spanish in her writings. Notably, however, she did not understand German, the native tongue of her father and her husband (Harris Newmark 224–25; Engh 75; Myer J. Newmark 232–33; Mrs. H. Newmark, "Echoes from Foreign Shores" Vol. 2, Aug. 4, 1887).

At age seventeen, Newmark married her first cousin, Harris, who had arrived from Prussia in 1853 and started his business career in LA as a clerk in the store of his older brother. By the time of their wedding, Harris had his own clothing store and had laid the foundation for what eventually would be the largest wholesale grocery firm in the city. Sarah's father officiated at the wedding, which was held in the family home about a block from the central Plaza, where Harris and Sarah resided until 1860. Their wedding guests included schoolmates of Sarah's and other early American and European pioneers whose ambitions had brought them to Los Angeles, Jews and non-Jews, typical of social occasions among Gold Rush and post Gold Rush era immigrants (Harris Newmark 224).

In contrast to the frequent relocations of her childhood, Newmark raised her own family primarily in one place, Los Angeles. Between 1859 and 1881, she bore eleven children but eventually lost six of them before they reached the age of ten. Despite epidemics, droughts, floods, banditry, racially motivated violence, and the existence of only embryonic educational, religious, and public safety institutions, the Newmarks achieved economic security and social mobility on the multicultural California frontier.

Contemporary historians have recognized for some time now that the mixing of diverse peoples served as a significant component in the gradual creation of the American West (see, for example, White). One view suggests that, especially with the influx of immigrants from Asia, Latin America, and Europe provoked by the Gold Rush, the West was characterized by "a raw cosmopolitan world-centeredness" (Rischin, "Jewish Experience in America" 32). The presence of immigrant and American-born Jews added religious diversity to the mix and another set of influences upon the social and economic possibilities of that frontier. Nineteenth-century California, with its flexible mingling of peoples, colonial legacies, and cultural norms, allowed the promise of cosmopolitanism to contend with the impulse of provincialism at least until the Spanish-Mexican borderland was fully incorporated into the American nation in the aftermath of "the great boom" of the 1880s.[4]

By that time, the Newmarks were well-established members of the elite citizenry of Los Angeles, along with other Jewish and non-Jewish ground-floor beneficiaries of the region's agricultural expansion, rising land values, and connection to the rest of the US via the railroad. They were extensively engaged in a diverse assortment of civic, religious, and economic institutions. Typical of Jewish women and men in the West, Sarah and Harris were active in both Jewish and non-Jewish charities and associations. They were among the founding families of Congregation B'nai B'rith, a traditional synagogue that underwent modernization under Harris's leadership in 1884. Like many middle-class American women of the period, Sarah was involved mainly in philanthropies that aided widows and orphans, including three different women's benevolent associations, the first non-Catholic orphans' home in LA, and a relief organization for Civil War Union veterans and their families (*Annual Report* 16). Their broad social circle and the prestigious status they were able to achieve were a product of the diversity and tolerance that marked the nineteenth-century American West.

Despite an antisemitism that was "endemic throughout the rural West," California's urban centers, especially San Francisco and Los Angeles, were experienced by their Jewish residents as "more tolerant" than cities in the East (Dinnerstein 50–51).[5] By 1880, some eight percent of the total US Jewish population lived in the West, thousands of miles away from their co-religionists and older, more established communities in the Northeast and the South (Rischin, "Jewish Experience in America" 34). Jewish immigrants, like others from Europe, were part of the economic and civic leadership in the nineteenth-century West. Using skills in commerce to achieve economic mobility, Jewish immigrants were considered useful and resourceful members of Western communities. The acceptance and respect they were accorded were demonstrated most publicly in the widespread and frequent election of Jews to public office from the Gold Rush era until the 1890s (Pomeroy 194, 204–05).

While the Newmarks traveled in Europe, Los Angeles reached the apex of the boom of the 1880s. Growing from 11,000 people in 1880 to over 90,000 by 1887, the predominantly Mexican town had evolved from a Spanish pueblo to become a modern city of a size and influence of a sort that its boosters had long imagined. Tourism, fueled by railroad rivalries and land speculation, and fanned by imaginative sales campaigns, dramatically accelerated the urbanization and stratification of Los Angeles. The influx of midwestern Protestants changed the meaning of the cosmopolitanism of the city in which residents had taken pride for several decades. Previously, Los Angeles promoters had boasted about its progressive, industrious population drawn from many nations as evidence of its worldliness and sophistication and the absence of any dominant group as the harbinger of opportunity without prejudice (McPherson 37). In the 1880s, while many Angelenos still thought of themselves as cosmopolitan, that is, open to many cultures and nationalities, newspapers and boosters began to privilege the American nativism rising up elsewhere, a direct reflection of the increasingly American-born Protestant character of the population. A history written in 1888 by two leading citizens captured this changing sensibility in three sentences:

> Los Angeles is cosmopolitan. Almost every nation under the sun is represented. The genuine American, who talks plain English with Yankee modifications, is the controlling element whenever he asserts himself... (Lindley and Widney, unnumbered 17)

In the 1890s, class agendas and social discrimination would join racial bigotry as the shapers of the rising city. While overt antisemitism did not arrive in LA until the twentieth century, Jewish Angelenos were well aware of discrimination in the US and oppressive policies and violence in Europe against their co-religionists.[6] Such conditions made elite Jews self-conscious of their sense of distinctiveness. Despite having deep roots in local communities, they continued to be anxious about their future as part of American society. The Newmarks returned to a city thoroughly incorporated into that society, a fact that made the participation of its minority citizens—including Jews who were often placed in the foreigner category no matter their birthplace—somewhat variable at best and non-existent at worst. While Sarah Newmark revised her European diary, her city was just then entering a five-decade period when Jews were to be excluded from public leadership, despite the fact that for the previous forty years they had routinely held elected office. The "beautiful, new and refined Anglo-Saxon part of town" was growing rapidly in size, becoming a point of particular pride for the town's boosters ("Los Angeles: First Impressions" 3).

NEWMARK'S GRAND TOUR

On the last day of April 1887, Newmark set off from Los Angeles with her husband, Harris, and their two youngest children, Marco and Rose, "to visit Europe for health and pleasure."[7] After traveling north by train to San Francisco, then east to New York City, they sailed across on the mail steamer, *La Normandie*. Joining them on board ship and for various portions of the tour were Newmark's sister, Harriet Meyer, and niece, Rosalie Meyer. Landing in France, they were met by Newmark's brother, Myer, his wife and two children, and a governess for the children, simply known to all the travelers as "Fraulein" (Mrs. H. Newmark, "Echoes from Foreign Shores" Vol. 1, May 1, 1887 and May 23, 1887).[8]

The Newmarks visited nearly every continental European capital, taking in the major sights of art, cultural, national history, and natural beauty suggested by the Baedeker guidebooks regularly used by American tourists.[9] In addition to France, they traveled to several regions of imperial Germany, Denmark, Sweden, Switzerland, Italy, Austria, the Netherlands, England, Scotland, and Ireland. They had extended stays at two resorts, one in the German state of Westphalia and the other in Italy.

The Newmarks routinely took walking or carriage tours of every city and village they visited, making a point to survey the homes of the wealthy as well as the poor section, which often was the Jewish quarter. They stopped in synagogues both as tourists and worshippers. While the Newmarks departed from the Baedeker recommended grand tour itinerary by occasionally adding tours of Jewish sites, generally these excursions were recorded with language, level of detail, and context similar to entries about other sightseeing events.[10] Out of over 370 entries, twenty-one narrated apparently intentional visits to Jewish synagogues, quarters, and cemeteries, most of which were part of broader tours of the city in which they were located.[11] Only the trip to Grajewo, the Jewish shtetl across the Russian border, stood out as being an unusual addition to the itinerary. That distinction was thrown into stark relief by the differences between Newmark's contemporary diary version and her later journal version of the visit.

Family was central to the Newmarks' itinerary in Europe and to Sarah's record of the trip. For much of the trip, they were accompanied by extended family. Myer, Sarah's brother who served as US Consul in Lyons, along with his French-born wife, were companions and guides to several cultural venues.[12] Their children were playmates for the younger Newmarks. The Newmarks spent four weeks in Loebau, the hometown of Harris, visiting the homes of various aunts and uncles. Relatives of their sons-in-law extended them hospitality in Paris, Stuttgart, Basle, and other cities. They took news and gifts to relatives of old friends in Los Angeles. Sarah Newmark shared these details in regular correspondence with her adult children who had remained at home: three married daughters and an eldest son whose marriage in July 1888 would bring the tourists back to California. The letters home consisted of pages of Newmark's diary, contemporaneous accounts of the sights, people, and experiences that filled the days of the tourists.

Newmark's record of the trip took shape in three stages, with a diary at the center. Her routine apparently was to jot brief notes about a given day's activities in a small notebook she carried. Then, in the evening or the next day, she wrote a more detailed account of the events on pages of letter copybooks. According to her husband, "with almost painful regularity," Newmark "entered her impressions and recollections of all she saw" (Harris Newmark 565). In these accounts, she included verbatim passages from the Baedeker guide as well as her personal impressions and reactions. In 1890, Newmark transcribed by hand entries from eight of the nine letter copybooks.[13] With varying degrees of revision, she copied the original diary entries into eight matching bound volumes, each of which was embossed on the spine with the title, "Echoes From Foreign Shores Mrs. H. Newmark" and the volume number. The diary preserved in the letter copybooks was the most complete record as well as the closest in time to Newmark's experiences, while the transcribed journal was a memorial to the trip, a result of reflection and distance.[14]

Since Newmark's children were the recipients of the original diary pages in the form of letters and the subject of the dedication of the transcribed journal, audience is significant in considering the differences between the two records. For Newmark, writing for her children may have liberated her from the expectations of conventional travel narratives and encouraged her to include material of particular relevance or interest to her family. In privileging her role as a mother, Newmark was claiming the right to speak out in a manner that she thought appropriate for a nineteenth-century woman and mother. While the original diary-letters may have been a way to help the adult children feel a part of the family excursion, the later journal became a way for Newmark to instruct all her children on how to be a part of America. In a modern form, it was an ethical will, a Jewish tradition in which parents bequeathed to their children their most cherished values.

A TWICE-TOLD JOURNEY

On June 21, 1887, while visiting family in the city of Lyck in the German state of Prussia, the tourists journeyed by carriage across the Russian frontier to the village of Grajewo.[15] The traveling party consisted of Sarah, Harris and their son Marco, Myer, Sophie and their son Henry, and at least two carriage drivers.[16] The clear, singular purpose of the trip was to see the people and institutions of Grajewo. In contrast to entries about other excursions, neither version narrating this trip contained descriptions of scenery, monuments, peasants in the countryside, or famous events. Rather, Grajewo was the object and the central subject. As Newmark's description implied, Grajewo probably was overwhelmingly Jewish, a market town with limited industry.[17] According to historical maps, it apparently was the shtetl nearest to Lyck, suggesting a possible geographic explanation for Newmark's comment that "this was our only chance of visiting Russia." Even convenient proximity, however, begs the question: why were wealthy American Jews interested in such a place?[18]

Eastern European family roots suggest one possible explanation: the Newmarks were curious about the world their ancestors had left behind. Joseph Newmark, the first to immigrate to America, was the son and grandson of respected Polish Hassidic Jews (Leo Newmark 19).[19] Those Newmarks who remained in Europe lived in a region that in the eighteenth century, and then again in the twentieth century, was ethnically and politically Polish. In between, the area came under Prussian rule and German replaced Polish as the official language. The descendants of Rabbi Abraham and Reb Meyer (Joseph Newmark's grandfather and father, respectively) embraced modernity by learning German, then by leaving Prussia for America. In the US, they became German Jews even before a unified German nation existed. For the American Newmarks and their "German Jewish tradition, . . . depth of [their] pride exceeded the length of [their] lineage" (Kramer, "A Commentary," in Leo Newmark 95).[20]

The Newmark family's spiritual and physical journey from East to West was a common one for European Jews as Enlightenment ideas, modernity, and emancipation spread through the continent in the eighteenth and nineteenth centuries. In the wake of wars and imperialist ventures, national borders and identities changed even as residents stayed put, making grandparents Polish Jews, parents Prussian Jews, and children German Jews. As with many Jewish immigrants from central Europe, the Newmarks who came to the United States privileged their German cultural identity, discouraged their American-born children from the use of Yiddish, and modernized their religious customs to better acculturate in their new home.[21]

Both narrations of the trip to Grajewo recorded an instance of privilege being exercised, unarticulated circumstances hovering around the edges, and a young boy puzzling over the concerns of the adults in the party. Both versions noted that spontaneous crossings of the Russian border were discouraged by visa requirements, yet neither version offered any explicit explanation of the motivations for the trip nor for the travelers not obtaining the necessary permission to cross. In both versions, Newmark clearly recorded her disgust for the "Polish" Jews in the marketplace and "Beth Midresh" and her admiration of the "tidy" Jews in an elastics factory. She left virtually unchanged a description of her fear of the "touch" of "dirty filthy street urchins," a fear that confused her nephew and was left unexplained in the written records. Given the legacy of the western Jewish antipathy toward eastern European Jews, Newmark's unease may have stemmed from a more abstract, but nevertheless, real fear—the "touch" of association with backward Jews, a reminder of the tenuousness of the modern Jew's position in contemporary society (Meyer 35; Berrol 151). Such consistencies across the two versions only serve to highlight the significant differences between the diary entry and the later journal version of the trip. Given the same author and same audience, an accounting of the variance between the versions suggests Newmark's changing perspective on her own Jewish and class identities in the emerging Los Angeles metropolis.

Newmark's first version of the trip showed her to have a sense of attachment, albeit an uncomfortable one, to the Jews of Grajewo. She used inclusive language ("our people") and she candidly expressed her embarrassment and shame about these examples of Jews and Judaism. In her revised narrative of the trip, Newmark substituted a sense of detachment, disassociating herself from the Polish Jews by deleting the inclusive language and candor. She went even further, though, by inserting a misleading motive that privileged an American identity. While the first version made it clear that the trip to Grajewo was planned and deliberate, the revised version implied it was more spontaneous and casual. In the original version, Newmark reflected an extremely negative opinion of the Polish Jews, while in the revision she tempered her language even as she created more distance between them and herself. Between 1887 and 1890, it became more important to Newmark to present herself as a modern, empowered American than as a part of an ancient people and religion.

To convey an impression that the trip to Grajewo was a casual visit similar to other tourist excursions, Newmark revised the original diary version by adding new phrases, deleting whole sentences, and changing key gerunds. She made these changes in the journal version to discourage association of the Newmarks with Polish Jews, and to emphasize her and her family's possession of standing as modern, privileged Americans. While the diary version conveys Newmark's revulsion at the sight and circumstances of Polish Jews living in Grajewo, the journal documents her desire to sever any connection possible through links of family history and religion to such backward, low-class people. To reinforce to her children that their future security and opportunities lay in attachment to their class and national identities and a modern attitude about their religion, Newmark erased her own initial frankness and embarrassed sense of commonality with the Grajewo Jews. The revised version makes the Newmarks tourists who visited a village in Russian Poland out of simple curiosity and convenience, demonstrated their American know-how in getting around ineffective bureaucratic rules, took note of the competing impulses of tradition and modernity, and returned with their appetites satisfied.

Consistently in the diary, Newmark did not explain motives or inspirations for her itinerary. In the case of the revised version of the Grajewo entry, however, she edited it to suggest motives of convenience and curiosity about Russia, a rather naive set of motives for traveling to a country where official actions towards Jews had grown increasingly more oppressive in the 1880s.[22] Given Newmark's long-standing communal and philanthropic engagement in Los Angeles, a plausible alternative explanation could have been concern about the conditions of Russian Jewry and a desire to aid her co-religionists in some way. No such motive was stated in either version. Instead, it seems that Newmark sought to dampen any hints that their journey to Grajewo had personal significance. To do so, she finessed the threat of Russian antisemitism and erased any evidence of her sense of affinity with the Jews in the Russian Pale.

The threat of Russian antisemitism was generalized from a condition that made travel "very troublesome for our people" to a bureaucratic bother for all foreigners when Newmark did not transcribe the phrase "our people" (Sarah Newmark, Diary #2, June 22 [1887]). She reduced the importance of reaching their destination with some key additions to the original diary entry that implied a lack of foresight and stressed the roles of chance and American identity in reaching Grajewo. Having "neglected to have" their passports appropriately endorsed by the Russian Consul, the tourists risked not being able to cross the Russian border, a risk not worth mitigating beforehand by getting the necessary permit. However, as Myer Newmark "luckily had with him" his

American Consul passport, they were allowed to continue on their way. By adding key adjectives, Newmark clarified that, while theoretically it was the "Russian" Consul who controlled their passage, in reality it was the "American" Consul who secured it (Mrs. H. Newmark, "Echoes from Foreign Shores" Vol. 1, June 21, 1887). Passing over the border as Americans with some official status, the Newmarks overcame the restrictions provoked by their religious identity. In the revised version, possession and assertion of an *American* identity became the key to their freedom of movement, literally and figuratively their ability to "pass" into and out of places of their choice.

A key change of a gerund made clear the choice that Newmark saw upon reflection about the excursion into the Pale. In the diary, she described the trip as "the only chance we have of *being* in Russia" (Sarah Newmark, Diary #2, June 22 [1887]; emphasis added). In the journal, she changed that phrase to "our only chance of *visiting* Russia" (Mrs. H. Newmark, "Echoes from Foreign Shores" Vol. 1, June 21, 1887; emphasis added). Given her initial anxiety, revulsion, and embarrassment, Newmark may well have felt a sense of what her existence in the village could have been, had her father not immigrated. By the time she came to transcribe the entry into the journal, she was well removed, and pointedly extended that remove, from Grajewo. She had exercised a choice to be an American tourist, not a visitor with a common cultural Jewish identity with the people of the village and all that represented.

Newmark made another set of editorial choices that reinforced her own distance from Grajewo and, by implication, imposed that distance on her children as well. She deleted phrases and sentences that conveyed any sense of a shared identity with the Polish Jews. The final journal version was devoid of the phrase "our people," used twice in the original diary entry. Further, Newmark discarded the two most explicit and extended expressions of the anxiety provoked by such associations. In one, she conveyed her expectations about the people of the village and her determination that the hired German governess not "see such a beastly set of our people as I knew were here." In the other, she summarized the impact of the encounter, taking an ironical tone even as she admitted a painful truth: "if ever I was ashamed of my religion, it was while visiting the delightful village of 'Grajewo.'" Embarrassed at the prospect and shamed in the retrospect, Newmark revealed anxiety over possible taint by association. By excising these personalized links and personal emotions, she obscured further the possibility that the Newmarks traveled there out of a sense of ethno-religious fraternity, thus providing a basis for association. She also asserted a lack of identification, an exercise in detachment that gave her children no hint of connection, however distant in time and geography, with "the lowest class of the Polish Jew" to which most of the village's inhabitants belonged (Sarah Newmark, Diary #2, June 22 [1887]).

Newmark modernized the language of the diary entry, offering an example to her children on acculturation, just as she continued her efforts at disassociation and detachment. She dropped or changed Yiddish and German words found in the initial version, using words more familiar and acceptable to English-speaking Americans. For example, she changed "shule" to "synagogue." She altered her initial adjective for the Polish Jews from "beastly" to "filthy." That alteration brought her description in line with a more common stereotype of the Polish Jew, while at the same time it created a clear contrast with the "tidy" and productive Jews of the elastics factory.[23] The change in adjectives also toned down the hyperbole of Newmark's diary entry, making her reaction less infused with anxiety while maintaining a sharp and critical distinction between herself and the Polish Jews.

As mentioned earlier, the Newmarks visited a number of Jewish quarters over the course of their time in Europe. None evoked the emotionalism, anxiety, or detachment found in Newmark's initial and later narrations of the Grajewo visit. The trip was personal and the implications of that fact were unsettling to Newmark miles away and years later. The Jewish focus of the diary version became unseemly, perhaps even untenable, in a Los Angeles embracing class, religion, and race as the determinants of respectability, acceptability, and mobility. Perhaps several goals were in mind as Newmark reconsidered that entry. Obscuring any potential association of the Newmarks with poor, backward Jews could have served to preserve her class status. The privileging of a modern American identity in the journal version was consonant with the emerging social standards of Los Angeles and evidence of her confidence in the value of American nativity. Furthermore, such preference for the modern was consistent with her rejection of traditional Judaism that began before her journey abroad. In revising her record of visiting Grajewo, and in the process revising the memory and meaning of the trip, Newmark repositioned herself, and by extension, her children, in the new Los Angeles social hierarchy.

CONCLUSION

After the trip to Grajewo, Newmark recorded many more visits to Jewish quarters and synagogues as they traveled Europe. She often remarked on the crowded and narrow streets of old ghettos, the poor Christians and Jews who occupied those sections, and the "old-fashioned" Orthodox style of Sabbath and holiday services. Occasionally she noted the Jewish population and number of synagogues of a given city, in an almost boastful way. In these other diary entries, Newmark seemed to be comfortable with her subjects even if they were unfamiliar. Only with her renditions of the Grajewo excursion do we find palpable apprehension related to a Jewish site. With them, we see a wealthy American Jewish woman experiencing the on-going need to claim, shape, and refine those identities, efforts necessitated by the limits of tolerance and the meanings of difference in the nineteenth century.

As cosmopolitan, that is, diverse California came to be seen as socially flawed rather than socially fluid, Jewish Angelenos were faced with choices about identity previously unnecessary to their incorporation and inclusion in the general community. In particular, class was becoming a critical distinction, and it would be conflated with religion and race, as the population Los Angeles grew proportionately more Protestant and Anglo.

Social change in Los Angeles occurred in the broader context of rising nativism and nationalism and the emergence of modern antisemitism. The last third of the nineteenth century saw "the Jewish Question" looming over both America and Europe. While Jews in America had achieved remarkable economic success and social integration, those achievements were tempered by ambivalent, often conflicting American attitudes towards Jews. As one scholar has noted, "many Americans were both pro- and anti-Jewish at the same time" (Higham 122).

In revising a travel diary for the benefit of her children, Sarah Newmark reflected the anxieties raised by these social realities and offered a response through reinvention and realignment of her and their identities. She modeled her view of Grajewo in a manner that allowed herself to maintain a significant degree of social detachment, which in turn served to benefit her sense of superior social standing. Newmark's lesson to her children followed a proven formula, embodied in a legacy that had led a Jewish family to the California frontier where they could be "real Americans," who could view a Russian Polish village not as part of their heritage but simply as an exotic if rather distasteful tourist stop.

Appendix A

Entry in letter copybook—the diary:

Tuesday June 22nd

This morning spent at Natalie's, her little ones are so [unreadable].[24] This afternoon we took carriages and drove over to Russia, to a place called "Grajewo." We had a good deal of trouble to pass, as no foreigners are ~~not~~ allowed to pass without a special permit from the Consul, our passports from Washington would not do, unless certified by him, however upon Uncle Myer showing his passport as a Consul, we were allowed to pass.[25] Well such a sight as met our gaze, when we reached the village, I cannot describe, most of the inhabitants are the lowest class of the Polish Jew, the market place was crowded with them. They are about as beastly a set as I have ever seen, with their long coats and greasy locks, but all of the men, with the "zitses" & "Alfaconfis" [?] hanging below their vests. We first visited a "fabrik" where all sorts of elastic goods are made such as garters, suspenders, etc are made. The parties that keep it are very nice respectable people, they showed us over every department, all the employees are Jews and looked pretty tidy. We made some few purchases, then left and visited the "Beth Medrish," well that was a sight, it was furnished something like a shule [sic], only that the benches had tables before them. At these sat men of various ages, poring over and studying from huge old hebrew volumes. The faces and the books, alike rather black and dirty. The men looked as if they were half starved. Near the entrance was a room which looked like a dark hole wherin [sic] sat an old man, teaching the young children of course hebrew [sic]. From here we visited the shule [sic]. We were followed thither by a large crowd of dirty filthy little urchins, I was quite uneasy, for fear some of them might touch us and that we might take home more than we bargained for. Henry asked us what sickness these people had, that we were afraid of catching. I did not take darling Rosa[26] [sic] as in the first place I knew we would get home very late, and secondly, I did not want the governess to see such a beastly set of our people as I knew were here. The shule [sic] was empty so there was nothing much to see. After this we drove out to see the depot, which is a very nice one. Here I took a glass of tea, the others did not care for any. We then left this sweet pure little village and wended our way homewards. We reached an inn at about eight o clock, where dear Natalie had a nice supper laid out, she brought it with her, also a servant to attend it, and I can tell you we all did justice to the meal. We left here about half past nine, and went once more on our way. We reached Lyck at about half past eleven all quite tired out, but we would not take a good deal for the novel sights we had seen, as this was the only chance we will have of being in Russia, as it seems to be very troublesome for our people to travel that country, nor do I wonder at it, for if ever I was ashamed of my religion it was while visiting the delightful village of "Grajewo" (Sarah Newmark, Diary #2, June 22 [1887]; item #34).[27]

Appendix B

Entry in transcribed bound volume—the journal:

Tuesday, June 21, 1887. Lyck

This morning spent at Natalie's. This afternoon took carriages and drove to a place called "Grajewo" a village in Russian Poland. We had a good deal of trouble to pass over the frontier, as no foreigners are allowed without a special permit from the Russian Consul, our passports from Washington would not do unless certified by him, and this we had neglected to have done, however upon uncle Myer showing his pasport [sic] as an American Consul, which he luckily had with him we were allowed to pass. Well such a sight as met our gaze when we reached the village, I cannot describe. Most of the inhabitants are the lowest class of Polish Jews. The market place was crowded with them. They are about as filthy a set, as I have ever seen, with their long coats and greasy locks. We first visited a factory where all sorts of elastic goods are made, such as garters suspenders etc. The parties that own this are very nice respectable people. They showed us through every department, all the employees are Jews and looked pretty tidy. We made some purchases, then left, and visited the "Beth Medrish." Well that was a sight! It was furnished something like a synagogue, only that the benches, had tables in front of them. At these sat men of various ages, poring over and studying from huge old hebrew volumes, the faces and books alike rather black and dirty. The men looked as if they were half starved. Near the entrance to this place, was a room, which looked like a dark hole, wherein sat an an [sic] old man, teaching the young children. From here we went to the synagogue we were followed through the streets by a large crowd of dirty filthy little urchins we were quite uneasy for fear that some of them might touch us and that we might take home more than we bargained for. Henry asked us very innocently what sickness these people had that we were afraid of catching? In the synagogue there was not much to see, as there was no service going on. After we left here, we drove to the depot, which is a very fine one, here I took a glass of tea, (genuine Russian). We then left this sweet, pure little village? and wended our way homeward. At eight O clock, we reached an inn, where Natalie had a nice supper laid out, and I must say we all did ample justice to the meal, which was provided for us. We left here about half past nine, and reached Lyck two hours later, all quite tired out, but we would not take a good deal, for the novel sights we had seen. This was our only chance of visiting Russia, as it seems it is very troublesome to ~~visit~~ travel in that country (Mrs. H. Newmark, "Echoes from Foreign Shores," Vol. 1, June 21 1887; item #6).[28]

Notes

1. The author would like to thank Janice Reiff, Kathryn Norberg, her classmates in the 2005 UCLA Social History seminar where this paper originated, David N. Myers, William Deverell, Bruce Zuckerman, and the *AR* reviewers for their insightful criticisms and editorial suggestions, as well as Stephen Aron and Naomi R. Lamoreaux for on-going conversations about the broader issues raised here. Research for the paper was supported by the Autry National Center-UCLA Summer Fellowship.
2. The two versions are: (1) Mrs. H. (Sarah) Newmark, "Untitled Travel Diary." Referred to in the text as "the diary"; (2) Mrs. H. Newmark, "Echoes from Foreign Shores." Referred to in the text as "the journal."
3. The Pale of Settlement was the legally mandated region of residence for most Jews within the Russian empire. Beginning in 1882, Jews were forced to leave rural areas of the Pale and reside in towns such as Grajewo. "Shtetl" is a Yiddish word meaning "little town/village." Newmark never used the word in relation to Grajewo, and it is unclear how much Yiddish she knew, though she seemed to have known at least a few words based on entries in her diary.
4. "The great boom" of the 1880s was the most spectacular and influential of the land booms that shaped Southern California in the nineteenth century. The population of Los Angeles grew five-hundred percent in less than a decade as settlers and speculators alike sought to take advantage of the break-up of the large ranchos that unleashed a torrent of undeveloped acreage. More than any other single event, the great boom made Los Angeles a modern metropolis. The classic work on the boom is Dumke's *The Boom of the Eighties in Southern California*.
5. Following the rationale and usage of philosopher Emil Fackenheim and historian Yehuda Bauer, I do not capitalize or hyphenate the term "antisemitism" when referring to the modern, racialized, pseudo-scientific version of anti-Jewish ideology and behavior, as there is no "Semitism" to be against or opposite. Modern antisemitism as a political ideology and movement began when German Wilhelm Marr coined the term in his book, *The Way to Victory of Germanicism over Judaism*, and founded the "League of Anti-Semites" in 1879.
6. See Cohen for a discussion of national awareness and the following *Los Angeles Times* articles for local reports: "The Jewish Question in Russia"; "The Persecution of the Jews"; "In Foreign Lands: An Outbreak against Jews Quelled"; "Attacking the Jews"; "An Exodus of Jews."
7. Quoted phrase from an article about a surprise send-off party for the Newmarks, "A Pleasant Occasion."
8. "Fraulein" was the term used throughout the diary and journal by Newmark in referring to the German-speaking woman in charge of the children. Other than the fact that she was German and seemed familiar to the family before their meeting in Paris, nothing else is known about the governess.

9. "Baedeker" became synonymous with "guidebook" in the nineteenth century, as the German publishing firm of that name produced a vast number of guides to European countries. Newmark apparently relied on the real thing, as evidenced by her routine copying of key phrases and passages from the guidebooks into her diary entries. For more about Baedeker guides, see Koshar.
10. Typical was Newmark's recounting of a tour of Frankfort, which began with a visit to a cathedral, continued with a carriage ride past the birthplace of the founder of the Rothschild banking dynasty, a stop in the "old Synagogue, and the house where Goethe the poet was born, also the monuments of Goethe and Gutenberg," and concluded with driving around "to see the elegant residences, that the city contains" (Mrs. H. Newmark, "Echoes from Foreign Shores" Vol. 2, Aug. 14, 1887).
11. Newmark recorded an additional sixteen occasions when she and other family members attended religious services at synagogues. The twenty-one occasions referenced here clearly were not of a religious nature.
12. Myer J. Newmark had been appointed Consul to Lyons, France, in 1885 by Grover Cleveland, and from that date lived in Europe for some ten years. A diary entry referred to Myer as "Ex United States Consul," so he may not have been an active consul at the time of the Grajewo visit (Mrs. H. Newmark, "Echoes from Foreign Shores" Vol. 7, April 17, 1888).
13. The transcription project ended with only a small portion of the eighth and none of the ninth letter copybook entered into the bound volumes. No explanation has been found about the unfinished project, although it may be related to the death in November 1890 of Newmark's youngest daughter, Rose, who had accompanied her parents and older brother Marco on the European tour.
14. See Appendix A for the full text of the diary entry on the visit to Grajewo and Appendix B for the full text of the journal version.
15. According to Baedeker's guide to Northern Germany, 1886 edition, Grajewo was located on the Russian border, about thirteen miles from Lyck. Grajewo, Lyck, and Loebau (where they had stopped earlier in the tour and where several generations of Newmarks lived) are all now within the national borders of Poland.
16. The diary entry explicitly stated that Sarah's daughter and the governess were not in the party; no mention was made of the daughter of Myer, who was with the family in Lyck.
17. Unconfirmed figures put the Jewish population of Grajewo at seventy-six percent in 1857 and still at thirty-nine percent in 1921 after large-scale migrations to the West and Palestine. See "Grajewo."
18. Given that a tour of an elastics factory was part of the visit to Grajewo, business interests could have motivated the trip. However, no evidence has been found to corroborate such a motive.
19. Hassidic Jews were members of a pietistic movement that originated in Eastern Europe in the eighteenth century and drew on Jewish mysticism, while elevating its

significance and introducing changes in traditional religious leadership and worship practices.
20. Kramer made the observation about Leo Newmark, a nephew of Sarah, who was born in San Francisco and was instilled with a deep sense of being the progeny of modern and respectable, i.e., German Jewish, stock, as were all the members of his generation and those of his parents' and Sarah's generation.
21. Emancipation for Jews in France and various other European states and the subsequent modernization of those communities created a division of experience and culture between western European Jews and their eastern European brethren (*Ost Juden*). "German-Jewish" immigrants to the U.S. carried this legacy of difference in the mid-nineteenth century. As westernized Jews came to see Polish and Russian Jews as backward and thus dangerous to their tenuous hold on the privileges of citizenship and social integration, efforts to mitigate the perceived danger included philanthropic projects designed to modernize the *Ost Juden* and assimilate them as quickly as possible. A vast literature discusses the "German versus Russian" division, as it came to be called, its impact in Europe, and its transference to the US. See for example Aschheim; Rischin, *The Promised City*; Sorkin; and Werthheimer.
22. Beginning in 1881, Jews in Russia were subjected to a series of pogroms and persecutions, events that were reported regularly in American newspapers that generally were sympathetic to the Jews and critical of the antisemitic sentiments and culprits behind the attacks. Concern about the perceived or actual numbers of refugees from Russia had become so inflamed in Prussia that Russian-Polish Jews were expelled first from Berlin and then from the rest of the state. In 1886 Russia required visas for both foreign and domestic travelers, a policy pointed out by a former US ambassador to the Russian Imperial Court in an interview with the *Los Angeles Times* April 17, 1886: 4.
23. "Karl Marx's description of Polish Jews as the 'dirtiest of all races . . . they multiply like lice' was not apt to provoke much disagreement amongst his peers" or most nineteenth-century German-Jewish Americans (Aschheim 60). Compare Newmark's description to that of an American diplomat's wife, a Christian, traveling in Russian in 1883: "There were quantities of dirty Polish Jews in every direction, all with their long caftans, greasy, black curls, and ear-rings" (Waddington May 17, 1883).
24. Natalie was a relative of Newmark, perhaps a sister-in-law or aunt, who lived in Lyck.
25. "Uncle Myer" was Newmark's brother, Myer J. Newmark. The use of "uncle" indicated that Newmark was writing to her children or at least intending to address them.
26. "Rosa" was Newmark's youngest daughter, Josephine Rose, who sometimes was called by her grandmother's name.
27. Punctuation, capitalization, and spellings retained from original.
28. Punctuation, capitalization, and spellings retained from original.

Works Cited

"An Exodus of Jews." *Los Angeles Times* March 23, 1886: 1.

The Annual Report of the Los Angeles County Pioneers of Southern California for the Years 1910–11. Los Angeles, 1911.

"A Pleasant Occasion." *Los Angeles Times* April 29, 1887: 1.

Aschheim, Steven E. *Brothers and Strangers: The East European Jew in German and German Jewish Consciousness, 1800–1923.* Madison, WI: Univ. of Wisconsin, 1982.

"Attacking the Jews." *Los Angeles Times* Aug. 18, 1883: 1.

Baedeker, K. *Northern Germany Handbook for Travellers.* 9th ed. Leipsic: Baedeker, 1886.

Berrol, Selma. "Germans Versus Russians: An Update." *American Jewish History* 73.2 (1983): 142–49.

Cohen, Naomi. "Anti-Semitism in the United States." *American Jewish History* 71.1 (1981): 5–9.

Diner, Hasia R. *The Jews of the United States, 1654 to 2000.* Berkeley and Los Angeles: Univ. of California, 2004.

Dinnerstein, Leonard. *Antisemtism in America.* New York: Oxford Univ., 1994.

Dumke, Glenn S. *The Boom of the Eighties in Southern California.* 6th ed. San Marino: Huntington Library, 1944.

Engh, Michael E. *Frontier Faiths: Church, Temple, and Synagogue in Los Angeles, 1846–1888.* Albuquerque, NM: Univ. of New Mexico, 1992.

"Grajewo." *Jewish Virtual Library.* The American-Israeli Cooperative Enterprise. Oct. 1, 2009 <http://www.jewishvirtuallibrary.org/jsource/judaica/ejud_0002_0008_0_07787.html>.

Higham, John. *Send These to Me: Immigrants in Urban America.* Rev. ed. Baltimore: Johns Hopkins Univ., 1984.

"In Foreign Lands: An Outbreak against Jews Quelled." *Los Angeles Times* June 1, 1883: 1.

"In High Office at Twenty-One: County's Youngest District Attorney Now Dead." *Los Angeles Times* May 11, 1911: II-1.

"The Jewish Question in Russia." *Los Angeles Times* Feb. 8, 1882: 1.

"Judge Taft Interview with the Ex-Minister to Russia." *Los Angeles Times* April 17, 1886: 4.

Koshar, Rudy. " 'What Ought to Be Seen': Tourists' Guidebooks and National Identities in Modern Germany and Europe." *Journal of Contemporary History* 33.3 (1998): 323–40.

Lindley, Walter and Widney, J. P. *California of the South.* New York, 1888. Los Angeles: Soule Steel, 1944.

Marr, Wilhelm. *Der Weg zum Siege des Germanentums über das Judentum* (The Way to Victory of Germanicism over Judaism). Bern: Oostenoble, 1879.

McPherson, William. *Homes in Los Angeles City and County, and Description Thereof with Sketches of the Four Adjacent Counties.* Los Angeles: Mirror and Job, 1873.

Southern California Chapter, Antiquarian Booksellers Association of America, 1961.

Meyer, Michael A. "Anti-Semitism and Jewish Identity." *Commentary* 88.5 (1989): 35–40.

Newmark, Harris. *Sixty Years in Southern California, 1853–1913, Containing the Reminiscences of Harris Newmark*. 4th ed. Ed. Maurice H. Newmark, Marco R. Newmark, and W. W. Robinson. Los Angeles: Dawson's Book Shop, 1984.

Newmark, Mrs. H. (Sarah). "Untitled Travel Diary." 1887. McDonalds's Stylograph: or Rapid Letter Copying Books labeled #1 through #9. Newmark Family Collection, MS.227. Los Angeles: Braun Research Library, Autry National Center of the American West.

Newmark, Mrs. H. "Echoes from Foreign Shores." Volumes 1–8. 1890. Newmark Family Collection, MS.227. Los Angeles: Braun Research Library, Autry National Center of the American West.

Newmark, Leo. *California Family Newmark: An Intimate Portrait*. Santa Monica: Stern, 1970.

Newmark, Myer J. Log Around the Horn—1852–1853. *Western States Jewish Historical Quarterly* 2.4 (1970): 227–45.

"The Persecution of the Jews." *Los Angeles Times* Feb. 19, 1882: 1.

Pierce, Edward L. "Los Angeles: First Impressions of a Stranger on Visiting the City." *Los Angeles Times* March 18, 1882.

Pomeroy, Earl. "On Becoming a Westerner: Immigrants and Other Migrants." *Jews of the American West*. Ed. Moses Rischin and John Livingston. Detroit: Wayne State Univ., 1991. 190–212.

Rischin, Moses. *The Promised City: New York's Jews, 1870–1914*. Cambridge, MA: Harvard Univ., 1977.

Rischin, Moses. "The Jewish Experience in America: A View from the West." *Jews of the American West*. Ed. Moses Rischin and John Livingstone. Detroit: Wayne State Univ., 1991. 26–47.

Sorkin, David. *The Transformation of German Jewry, 1780–1840*. Detroit: Wayne State Univ., 1999.

Waddington, Mary Alsop King. *Letters of a Diplomat's Wife*. New York: Scribner's, 1903.

Werthheimer, Jack. *Unwelcome Strangers: East European Jews in Imperial Germany*. Studies in Jewish History. New York: Oxford Univ., 1987.

White, Richard. *"It's Your Misfortune and None of My Own": A New History of the American West*. Norman, OK: Univ. of Oklahoma, 1991.

Postscript: The Western States Jewish History Archives

Gladys Sturman and David Epstein

The early history of the Jews of the American West might have been lost had it not been for the efforts of two remarkable men. Over many years, Dr. Norton Stern and Rabbi William Kramer engaged in painstaking research and diligent acquisition of materials. In the process, these pioneer historians painstakingly assembled a vast archive and founded the *Western States Jewish History Journal*, now in its forty-first year.

Across the United States and the world, there is an astonishingly rich repository of recorded information about, for example, the Jews who fled to New Amsterdam in 1654; about the German Jews who came to the United States in the Civil War era; and about the mass immigration of Eastern European Jews between the 1880s and 1920s. The majority of these Jews remained in the big cities, founded synagogues, service organizations and the great cultural and educational institutions that are so well known to us today.

But as Stern, an optometrist and principal of a synagogue Hebrew school, and Rabbi Kramer knew well, Jews also ventured all the way across the North American continent, traversing in relatively large numbers this vast country to reach the states and territories of the far West. They traveled in every imaginable manner: by wagon train across the prairies, by ship around Cape Horn and the tip of South America, by mule across the malarial Isthmus of Panama, then on board steamers sailing north up the Pacific coast. They came, as historian Doyce Nunis has said, for the same reasons everyone else came: "for economic opportunity, climate, health and romantic myth" (personal communication). Many came as miners or merchants due to the Gold Rush. They came, many as young unattached teenaged or younger boys, from European countries to escape discrimination and persecution; many could speak no English when they arrived.

The Jews who came West in the early days were not as religious as some of their fellow Jews. The more pious Jews were inhibited from traveling too far from the eastern cities because they could not be sure they would find kosher food, a mikvah, and other ritual amenities essential for their daily life. Most of the early Jewish pioneers to the far west felt they needed a synagogue only once a year for Rosh Hashanah and Yom Kippur. Such services were usually held in a home or empty store and led by the most knowledgeable person among them, using a printed Torah. Establishing synagogues was a low priority for these men. The most important issue for them was to take advantage of the opportunities presented them in the far West—especially opportunities that might not have been so readily available or socially acceptable in the more established eastern urban centers.

As is evident in several of the essays in this volume, these early arrivals played a major role in shaping the character and dynamism of the West. They created successful models in business, banking, politics, journalism, and culture. Most impressive was their success in maintaining their Judaism. Since synagogues were a low priority, the first Jewish institution in a Western town was usually a Jewish cemetery and burial society. As Norton Stern discovered, these cemeteries turned out to be invaluable sources for tracking regional Jewish history.

Norton Stern traveled throughout California taking pictures of tombstones in Jewish cemeteries. Armed with names and birth and death dates, he would then go to the local newspaper and meticulously search for references to the deceased. This Herculean effort was done without benefit of microfiche, let alone the Internet. As Stern researched articles, he found references to other Jews of the period or to other Jewish organizations, and he carefully noted (and usually photographed) these as well. Each step revealed yet another level of early Jewish history. The last step was to seek out the descendants of early pioneers. If he found family members, he would interview them and thereby add to the richness of the story.

When Stern began this quest he had to handwrite the interviews. The later use of a tape recorder would make the process faster and more efficient. As Cyril Leonoff, the Canadian editor of *Western States Jewish History Journal*, described this effort, Stern looked "through hundreds of haystacks for dozens of needles and for no other reason than the love of it" (personal communication).

In his single-minded pursuit of the stories and people of the western Jewish past, Norton Stern became a father of Jewish history of the American West. He and Rabbi Kramer amassed thousands of family pictures, photographs of stores, homes, and buildings, school pictures, and many other materials. They also accumulated a vast store of newspaper articles; interviews; letters dating back to the mid-nineteenth century; business receipts; membership and political lists; advertisements; government documents; and so on. In addition, they acquired a goodly number of diaries; photo albums; wedding invitations; a *tallis* bag made of burlap; early telephone directories; posters announcing High Holiday services; and business cards (including one of a cigar dealer that warns "Beware of Jewish Imitations").

After Norton Stern's death, Rabbi Kramer assumed the responsibility for maintaining the archives and publishing the *Western States Jewish History Journal*. He continued the journal for many years until his own health deteriorated, at which point he turned its management over to us. In the transition, we inherited over one thousand books plus about three hundred boxes of very loosely sorted archival material. We knew that each item would have to be examined and organized in some coherent fashion. Without organization, this massive collection would never be fully accessible to scholars, students, genealogists, and others.

Accordingly, we assembled a coterie of volunteer archivists. Norman and Mimi Dudley, who were retired from their professional archival careers at UCLA, gave us a basic how-to course, teaching us about process and materials. With their guidance we set to work.

Every piece of paper had to be examined individually, often with a magnifying glass because the photos had faded or because the newspaper pages were so fragile. All available information about content, context, or provenance was noted. It was painstaking work, invariably interrupted every few minutes by "You've got to hear this!" or "You've got to see this!" Some of the newspapers dating back to the 1800s were too fragile to unfold. We set these aside for professionals to handle. Photos had to be identified and labeled. Occasionally we would publish an unmarked picture to see if any of our readers could identify it.

Documents were carefully housed and information entered into a database for ease of retrieval. Once organized, the archives were donated to appropriate institutions to be available for research. The bulk of the written material, nearly two hundred finished archival boxes and thirty boxes yet to be completed, went to UCLA's Charles Young Library of Special Collections. Information on the history of the West that did not pertain to Jewish settlers was donated to the Autry National Center. Newspapers too fragile to open, as well as ephemera, letters, albums, film reels and such went to the Huntington Library. The addition of materials from this very large collection has made these institutions among the important libraries of the Jewish history of the American West.

What does all this material reveal? In some ways, it's far too soon to tell: the documents, books, photographs, and other materials await scholarly investigation, contemplation, and eventual publication. Yet some preliminary findings, gleaned from our hours-upon-hours of sorting, cataloging, and organizing, are warranted here. In the archives, we discovered letters, business records and news articles indicating that these early Jewish pioneers were not only successful in business, politics, journalism, cultural affairs, and finance, but that they contributed much to this new world of the far West as family members, religious figures, and role models.

Their success can be attributed to many reasons. Many were young when they arrived in the West and thus able to exist with the barest necessities. They also appear to have matched their ambitions with abstemious and frugal habits. The integrity of many stands out: as merchants, bankers, or other businessmen, they offered generous credit and financial aid. Many were trusted assayers. When you left your gold at the "Jew Store," it would be there when you came to claim it.

In a mining world of fairly random literacy, many a Jewish pioneer stood out in level of education; they put their reading and writing skills to work in keeping track of business inventories, loans, and the like.

As the West and our subjects matured, they became increasingly active in civil affairs; many became the pillars of local society: political leaders, attorneys, judges, legislators, peace officers, and otherwise. And while we need far more work on this topic, we suggest that the far West, at least the nineteenth century far West, exhibited less —and perhaps far less—anti-Semitic religious or ethnic hostility compared with the East Coast and the often far more intolerant European continent. This allowed western Jews a degree of freedom to dream and succeed to a remarkable and otherwise unprecedented degree in America, and this marks the West as particularly fertile land of opportunity for Jews.

To say the least, this archival work has been a labor of love for everyone involved. We are confident that we have rescued a treasure house of historical material and, with it, the life stories and legacies of an important group of early westerners. That is a gift rarely granted, and we are grateful for the chance to be a part of this ongoing history of our people.

Postscript: The Western States Jewish History Archives

Appendix

From this vast collection of material we have often pulled out what we like to call snippets; they provide a miniature glimpse of life for the early Jewish settlers, and it is perhaps of interest to reproduce a few of these here. Taken as individual moments in time and circumstance, or collectively as part of a much larger mosaic of history, these "snippets" evoke aspects of the rich cultural, social, and familial history of Jews in the far West.

SOME HAD TO DO WITH BUSINESS DEALINGS:
- June 23, 1882 from the *Los Angeles Times*: "Mr. E. Berman, of Bloomington, Illinois, an experienced watchmaker, has just arrived to take a position on the force of Platt and Page, the jewelers."
- August 24, 1882 from the *Los Angeles Times*: "People vs. Martin Weiss. For keeping a place where gambling with dice is permitted; jury waived; demurrer to complaint overruled; plead not guilty; case tried; defendant found guilty as charged; at request of defendant, sentence postponed until 9½ A.M. today."
- December 6, 1873 from the *Los Angeles Times*: "THE CASH STORE—Harris and Jacoby. These gentlemen, who own one of the best stock establishments in the City, have just received a shipment of new merchandise. There is hardly a thing you might ask for that cannot be found in their establishment."

  > Gents furnishing, Fancy Goods, Yankee Notions, Toys Musical Instruments, baby wagons, school books and stationery, cigars and tobacco, fresh garden seeds.

- October 19, 1860 from *The Weekly Gleaner*: "Mr. L. L. Dennery, formerly of this city [San Francisco], has associated himself with Mr. Willis, at San Bernardino, in the practice of the law, and, convinced of the integrity of Mr. Dennery, we wish the firm of Willis & Dennery success."
- February 1, 1860 from *The Weekly Gleaner*: "Betrothed—Leon L. Dennery and Jane Jacobs."
- April 22, 1876 from *La Cronica*: "We are publishing today the notice of Bernardo Salomon, tailor. His prices are not only the most modest in town, but he also colours all kinds of clothing and fixes carriage awnings."

SOME WERE CULTURAL:
- Los Angeles 1884 from the *Star*: "Los Angeles has acquired a really 'elegant' theater: Childs' Opera House. About this time, Al Levy took up his stand in front of the Opera House with his little push cart and his famous California oyster cocktails."

SOME HAD TO DO WITH RELIGION:
- July 17, 1857, a letter from M. Raphael to the *Weekly Gleaner* described the "soon-to-be erected synagogue in Jackson, Amador County. We thank all who donated to the structure for Jewish worship in the Mother Lode country."
- September 20, 1876: "Rosh Hashanah afternoon was spent in visiting, where out-of-towners renewed old acquaintances and families held pleasant reunions."
- September 20, 1865 from *The Hebrew*: "On Monday last, the respected wife of Mr. Simon Appel, a co-religionist, was received into the Holy Covenant by the Rev. Fr. Henry A. Henry. The lady has been married to Mr. Appel about a year, and her amiable qualities have endeared her to all who have had the pleasure of her acquaintance."

SOME HAD TO DO WITH RABBIS:
- April 15, 1887 from the *American Israelite*: "I have recently heard that the Rev. Dr. Schrieber has made a good speck in real estate. Good, I am glad if it is true, though I believe some people think it next thing to a crime for a minister to make a dollar."

SOME DEALT WITH DAILY LIFE:
- April 18, 1868 from the *Jackson Amador Dispatch*: "A woman named Celia Levy, keeper of a saloon in Portland (Ore.), was shot lately by a man named Charles Starr. She said Starr owed her $3, and commenced calling each other names, and it ended in shooting her through the left lung."
- June 6, 1883 from the *Los Angeles Times*: "Dr. Wise has been making some extensive improvements in his residence on Main Street. He has had the interior papered and frescoed and made use of the many aesthetic devices so fashionable at present. Altogether he has been to the expense of $3,700."

SOME HAD TO DO WITH POLITICS:
- March 24, 1855 from the *Weekly Chronicle*: "There is nothing in the law to prevent a Jew from holding office. It does not sound well here, with all our boast of freedom and liberality, to commence a crusade against that sect because they do not agree with our faith. They are citizens, no?"

SOME HAD TO DO WITH THE LAW:
- March 10, 1888 from the *Los Angeles Times*: "B. Solomon, the notorious 'fence', held to answer on charge of receiving stolen goods, spent last night in jail—his bail raised from $2,000 to $3,000 which he was unable to pay."

To be sure, these are but the briefest introduction to the fascinating history of Jews in California; yet, even their fleeting, momentary nature reminds us of the world that awaits the careful, patient researcher intent upon delving into the documentary, visual, and other records that bespeak the history of a people, a region, and a time.

From Civic Defense to Civil Rights: The Growth of Jewish American Interracial Civil Rights Activism in Los Angeles

Shana Bernstein

INTRODUCTION

Jewish Americans helped develop an interracial form of civil rights activism in Los Angeles during the 1930s, 1940s, and early 1950s. They were often a central organizing force behind interracial coalitions that appeared in Los Angeles during this period. Jewish Americans' interracial orientation was rooted in the 1930s, when they increasingly realized that they were not safe, even on the far west coast of the United States and an ocean away from Germany. Their realization sparked a new form of civic defense activism to protect themselves.

Los Angeles Jewish Americans' activism transformed during World War II, as they increasingly realized that they could protect themselves best by helping to protect others as well. They shifted from monitoring only their own safety to increasingly working in collaboration with other local and national minority groups to ensure the greater safety of all, specifically through the pursuit of greater civil rights. The Cold War only deepened this commitment, as Jews' quadruple fear of racial violence, ongoing discrimination, becoming red-baiters' targets, and the spread of communism led them to build alliances for self-protection and to fight communism.

This paper traces the Jewish community's increasing involvement in interracial civil rights struggles through one group in particular, the Community Relations Council, or CRC. By the mid 1940s, the CRC became known as the organized Jewish community's primary intergroup relations organization and played a crucial role in building alliances between the Jewish community and other minority groups.[1]

THE 1930s: FORMATIVE YEARS

Jews in Los Angeles had created a community infrastructure in earlier years, but before the 1930s they had few organizations which focused significant energy on defending their community. Nazi activities and other forms of rising domestically-rooted anti-Semitism in Los Angeles during the 1930s, though, sparked new action in a community that had done relatively little in the way of self-protection in previous decades. Local Jews realized the extent to which dangerous racial philosophies abroad and at home made them vulnerable even in the "City of Angels," far from Germany. This recognition marked the official beginning of the Los Angeles Jewish community's struggle to fight for its own rights and, later, for other minorities' rights.

Jewish Americans faced increasing exclusion and anti-Semitism during the 1930s, though conditions for them were more tolerable than they were for other Los Angeles communities, namely, African Americans, Mexican Americans, and Japanese Americans, the city's other three most prevalent minority groups. Jews' rights were never openly attacked in any "reputable quarter," according to historians Max Vorspan and Lloyd Gartner, and no significant public figure or major party spoke out against them. But despite this "façade of safety," a small group of local Nazis, including the numerous fascist organizations that were active in Los Angeles, like the German Bund, made their lives increasingly more difficult (Vorspan and Gartner 205).[2]

Publicity surrounding one particular incident revealed the anti-Semitic danger lurking in Los Angeles. On September 19 and 30, 1935, fascist sympathizers distributed approximately 50,000 copies of an anti-Semitic pamphlet around Los Angeles. They inserted the pamphlet in home editions of the *Los Angeles Times*, the largest newspaper in the Southern California region. They also posted them on Southern California telephone poles, slipped them under doors, left them on street corners, and tossed them into automobiles. The propaganda shocked many Jewish and other Los Angeles residents when they opened their morning paper and walked through their neighborhoods. Some *Times* employees apparently had sneaked it into the paper, allegedly without management's knowledge. The pamphlet claimed that Jews displayed "unspeakably bestial degeneracy." They supposedly had a "distinctly racial program" which called for "the seduction of a SHIKSE (any Gentile girl, young or unprotected)" and performed "lewd and lascivious acts . . . intended to introduce vice and perversions into the lives of small children." Among many other attacks, the pamphlet charged that Jews "have promoted a widespread contempt for the ordinary virtues of honor and honesty in business," and asserted that Jews owned the movies, radio, and many magazines and newspapers—which all was part of an attempt to control access to "our people" (American Nationalist Party, in McWilliams; see Pitt 8-9, 20; and Gardner 86-87).

The main threat to Los Angeles Jews, though, came in more "respectable" forms of anti-Semitism, especially from groups like the Ku Klux Klan that used so-called gentlemen's agreements to exclude Jews from home ownership and social groups in Los Angeles neighborhoods. Restrictive covenants completely closed many areas to Jews. Elite social and business clubs and even the Chamber of Commerce, which in earlier years had Jewish founders and officers, began to exclude Jews. Certain kinds of employment effectively barred them; jobs as lawyers, except in Jewish firms, were generally off-limits, as were public school teacher positions. Myths circulated on Los Angeles radio that Jews had caused the depression and war (Vorspan and Gartner 205-06).

Jewish community leaders called meetings to discuss this rising anti-Semitism. Out of one such meeting in 1933 sprang the Community Relations Committee (hereafter CRC)—called the Community Committee until 1941, the "civic protective" group which began as a watchdog agency to monitor local fascist and anti-Semitic activities. The realization that Hitlerism was not to be contained in Europe, the CRC's first executive secretary Leon Lewis emphasized, led to his organization's creation. "Profiting by the experience of our unfortunate co-religionists in Germany," Lewis explained to other Jewish community officials two years after the CRC's formation, "small committees in several of the larger cities [including Los Angeles] have operated quietly and efficiently since the early part of 1933 to stem a mounting wave of organized activity against the Jew [in the United States]" (Lewis, Letter to Hilborn). At the end of the CRC's first year, Lewis reflected upon the Los Angeles Jewish community's sudden awareness of the danger it faced. While "American Jews [had] been confronted with no serious problem of this character" in previous years, Lewis explained, "suddenly the inspiration of Hitlerism resulted in the mushroom growth of a movement" of anti-Semitism (Lewis, Memorandum).

Jewish community leaders originally formed the CRC to monitor and report on the activities of local groups perceived to be threats to Jews and to democracy more generally. Consequently, in its early years the CRC focused primarily on monitoring fascist and pro-Nazi groups like the Friends of New

Germany, the German American Bund, and the Silver Shirts, as well as other anti-Semitic and racist groups such as the KKK. The CRC strove in the 1930s to be a clearinghouse for anti-Nazi efforts. It gathered and processed information about such groups, and countered their propaganda through public education (Lewis, Letter to Mischel). Because Jewish community members believed that officials and the public were not aware or vigilant enough about the threats posed by these groups, they felt both a strong responsibility and a heavy burden for bringing their activities to the public's attention. The CRC sent spies to infiltrate Nazi and pro-German organizations' meetings, monitored their publications, followed their public activities, and gauged their influence throughout the city. Spies reported back to the CRC about Bund and Friends of New Germany members' activities, including what cars they drove, where they drove them, who they talked and associated with, and what they discussed at their meetings. The CRC developed relationships with publishers of local Jewish and other presses in an attempt to persuade them to monitor and expose the groups' activities in their newspapers. It also published extensive reports in the News Research Service, a publicity organization with close ties to the CRC. The CRC sponsored educational workshops. It also pressed law enforcement officials and politicians to meet with CRC members with the hope of increasing their vigilance. The CRC took credit for certain victories—for instance, for reducing the membership in the Friends of New Germany from 350 to 130 (Lewis, Summary of Operations).[3] The CRC became a main organization occupied with the defense, protection and civil rights of the Los Angeles Jewish community in the 1930s.

During the 1930s, and through the first decades of its existence, the CRC spoke for the many constituent organizations in the greater organized Jewish community of Los Angeles, which all represented a relatively small but growing community. Many members of the Jewish community living in East LA neighborhoods like Boyle Heights were working-class and immigrant, while those in central and western LA tended to be more middle-class and American-born. Between 1927 and 1941, greater Los Angeles's Jewish American population doubled from approximately 65,000 to 130,000 (Vorspan and Gartner 287). Many Los Angeles Jews, especially immigrants, had ties to radical organizations and ideologies, socialists as well as communists. These included organizations like the Jewish Peoples' Fraternal Order, a workers' group with communist affiliations and about 5,000 Southern California members. Many LA Jews affiliated through the numerous synagogues in LA, while others mainly identified through a growing Jewish secular community structure. Even the secular organizations were extremely diverse, ranging from the rather left-leaning American Jewish Congress to the more conservative American Jewish Committee.

CRC members were both Republicans and Democrats. It drew participation from a wide array of influential Jewish Los Angeles civic, business, and cultural leaders. Hollywood figures supported the CRC and participated in its activities to varying degrees, though for the most part they provided financial backing rather than day-to-day involvement. Prominent participants included the Warner brothers, Louis B. Mayer—MGM's president until 1951—Adolph Zukor—the founder of Paramount Pictures—and eventually Dore Schary—the screenwriter and producer who succeeded Mayer as MGM's president (Lewis, Letter to Pacht).[4] Business community representatives on the CRC included executives of large department stores such as the May Company and Bullocks and Barkers. Leaders of the Jewish legal community became especially active, including judges Harry Hollzer, Isaac Pacht, and Stanley Mosk. Prominent attorneys included representatives of Loeb and Loeb and Mendel Silberberg. Among the most influential members were Silberberg, Pacht, and Mosk. One of his contemporaries described Silberberg as a local "king maker" because of his political influence with people like Mayor Fletcher Bowron and even Republican Governor Earl Warren.[5] Pacht and Mosk were well connected, too. After serving as California Governor Culbert Olson's legal secretary until Earl Warren replaced Olson in 1942, Mosk became a Los Angeles County Superior Court Judge. He later became California's Attorney General (1958) and then a California Supreme Court justice (1964). Pacht, who became an important member of the Jewish community, as well as a prominent figure in interracial organizing efforts in the 1940s and 1950s, was appointed to the Los Angeles Superior Court in 1931 and to the State Board of Prison Directors in 1940. Because many of the CRC's members were connected to politicians and were influential judges, lawyers, and Hollywood people themselves, the organization had access to local and state political power.

Though the CRC claimed to speak for the Jewish community as a whole, it most directly represented certain elements of this community—especially its more middle-class and upper-middle-class segments. Arguably, it is difficult, if not impossible, for any one organization to represent a community as diverse as LA's Jewish community during the 1930s. But because the CRC spoke with the voice of the organized Jewish community and was often taken as such by the larger mainstream political and lay community, it held a certain authority.

Its actions mattered a great deal in Jewish Los Angeles, and eventually to a larger political and social world in the city, state, and even the nation.

WORLD WAR II: INTERRACIAL COLLABORATION BEGINS

Pearl Harbor and the United States' entry into World War II in 1941 marked a turning point for LA's Jewish American community as a whole, and for this important Jewish community organization in particular. The federal and local government's more active involvement in Nazi groups' activities, which officially became subversive once the United States entered the war against Germany, enabled the CRC to shift to other issues important to the Jewish community. Officials began arresting numerous Angelenos and charging them, as Nazis, with subversive activities. A federal grand jury indicted the former West Coast chairman of the German-American Bund and Silver Shirt member Herman Schwinn on charges of conspiracy and sedition. It also indicted Frank K. Ferenz, who had been distributing Nazi films, and Hans Diebel, the Aryan Book Store's operator ("6 Southland Folk Indicted as Seditious"; "More Sedition Cases Seen"). CRC members found themselves relieved of enough of this monitoring work to shift their focus from civic defense.

At the same time, CRC members increasingly realized that they could pursue their interests best by collaborating with other minority groups, who like themselves became increasingly visible in the city during and especially after the war. Los Angeles was transforming from a largely white Protestant city early in the century to one whose population by 1950 was approximately twenty percent minority, including mostly African Americans, Mexican Americans, Japanese Americans, and Jews.[6] Many of these diverse recent migrants came because of stories they heard about the sunny weather and the "good life" in this spacious city, as well as to take advantage of growing job opportunities, which the war brought to western cities like Los Angeles. Jewish Americans in the CRC now focused on building civil rights bridges with these other minorities and liberal "Anglos," which became their organization's main focus after 1941. By mid-1943, they increasingly discussed ways to strengthen relations with other minority groups, especially African and Mexican Americans. They offered assistance to groups like the Fellowship Center, which sought to establish a community center in eastern Los Angeles that would provide "some effective help . . . to the Negroes" (CRC, Minutes of Public Relations Subcommittee Meeting, April 29, 1943). Lewis and the CRC initiated a campaign with the County Committee for Interracial Progress to persuade local department stores to depict others than Anglo-Saxon, blue-eyed children in their Christmas displays (Lewis, Letter to Gleason). The Jewish Community Council (JCC), the umbrella organization for the organized Jewish community, encouraged its members to join the local Urban League to show support for its work and the black community (LA Jewish Community Council, Letter to members, February 7, 1944).

Jewish Americans often played key roles in interracial anti-discrimination efforts, which incorporated religious, labor, and industry leaders as well as representatives from communities like Mexican Americans and African Americans (LeBerthon).[7] The CRC, in particular, became one of the most active catalysts for civil rights coalition building. It used its members' powerful political and community connections to convince Mayor Bowron and other leaders to initiate race relations projects. Silberberg, Pacht, and other CRC members persuaded Mayor Bowron in 1945 to propose a Mayor's Community Relations Board to permanently counsel LA minority groups, help ease racial tensions in the Mexican and "Negro" communities, and deal with local anti-Semitism and anti-Catholicism. The ordinance ultimately failed in spite of Bowron's support, but it nevertheless marks an increase in Jewish interests in multiracial anti-discrimination efforts (Silberberg, Letter to Cooke).

The CRC's decision to team up with other minorities was neither easy nor unanimous. Community members wrangled with each other over the desirability of aligning with other, "worse off" minority groups. Their interracial involvement by the middle—and especially by the end—of the war represented a clear shift. In 1941, CRC members were reluctant to ally with African Americans. They debated joining African Americans also working to fight state employment discrimination by establishing a California race relations commission. Though many meeting attendees in principle supported legislation proposed by Augustus Hawkins, the African American Assemblyman, the dominant perspective that "we should not get behind so-called racial bills as Jews and classify ourselves with the colored group" triumphed. CRC members "unanimously opposed . . . the sponsorship of any legislation at this time."[8] While an aversion to publicly associating with such a clearly downtrodden group, given their own precarious status, explains some of Jews' resistance, prejudice against African Americans helps explain this resistance to cooperative efforts as well.

But by the end of World War II, the CRC and other Jewish organizations expressed a markedly different attitude towards building coalitions with other, more obviously marginalized minorities. The CRC's postwar stance on cooperating with African Americans to fight employment discrimination illustrates this shift. By the late 1940s the CRC listed establishing a statewide Fair Employment Practices Commission (FEPC) as a top priority. Isaac Pacht, the past president of the Los Angeles Jewish Federation Council and past chairman of the CRC, joined C. L. Dellums, a prominent leader of the African American labor and civil rights organization, the Brotherhood of Sleeping Car Porters, to co-chair a multiracial statewide organization formed to fight employment discrimination. The two secretaries of this committee, the California Fair Practices Committee, were Max Mont of the Southern California Jewish Labor Committee and Bill Becker of San Francisco's Jewish Labor Committee (Pitt 53). Observers credited both the African American and Jewish communities for initiating the effort, which others (Mexican Americans, Asian Americans, and whites) joined (Sherman).

THE COLD WAR: INTERRACIAL ACTIVISM CONTINUES

The Los Angeles Jewish community's heightened commitment to interracial coalition building continued during the early Cold War era. In one major example, the organized Jewish community, through the CRC, helped support the establishment of the first enduring civil rights organization for the largest urban Mexican-origin population in the United States, which still exists today. The Community Service Organization (CSO), a civil rights organization which served mostly Mexican-origin Angelenos but also all of the Eastside's diverse residents, emerged in 1947. It began as a Los Angeles organization but by 1963 had established thirty-four chapters across the Southwest, primarily in California, with over 10,000 paid members. The CSO was the first organization to broker relationships effectively between Los Angeles' Mexican American people and the city and county of Los Angeles, and it became the most successful Cold War-era organization for Los Angeles Mexican Americans. The bulk of the activism that created the impetus for the CSO emerged out of the Mexican American community, with the assistance of the Anglo activist Fred Ross.

But Jewish American community support was crucial to the CSO's survival in its early years. From 1947 to 1950 the bulk of its funding came primarily from the Los Angeles Jewish community. The CSO's executive director recognized the importance of the Jewish support, explaining that without the CRC's funding, the CSO could not operate the next year (CSO memo, April 18,1951; CRC Meeting Minutes, August 30, 1948; CRC Meeting Minutes, July

14, 1949). The Jewish Community, through the CRC, did more than provide financial assistance to the CSO. It consulted with the Mexican American community, through the CSO, on legal, political, and financial matters. The CRC shared its expertise in the field of community relations and organizations with Mexican Americans, as it also did from time to time with Japanese Americans and African Americans (Guzman; CRC Minutes, August 31, 1950). It helped the CSO achieve tax-exempt status, provided assistance for legal problems and court cases, helped find employment for Mexican American community members, and consulted with the CSO on starting children's camps and dealing with "youth problems" and "educational problems." It also worked with the CSO on police brutality issues, participating in activities to educate the LA police department on minority issues in the interests of preventing overuse of force. When the CSO pressured the police department to initiate a police training program on minority issues and treatment in 1949, the director of the CRC gave such a successful lecture that the academy asked him to return to conduct more (CRC Meeting Minutes of Committee on Agencies, October 21, 1949; CRC Meeting Minutes Subcommittee on CSO, August 31, 1950).

The CRC made cooperation with and support for the CSO a central project. Its members believed that the CSO's work was crucial to both the Mexican American and the Jewish American communities. As a memo explained, "The Staff Committee felt that this project carried the greatest impact ... of any project submitted to the CRC" (CRC, Memo August 13, 1948). The CRC's executive director Fred Herzberg similarly emphasized to CRC members the importance of their support for the CSO, which exemplified "grass roots democracy at its best" (Herzberg, Letter to CRC members). The CRC further urged Jewish community members to value this "extremely important operation [the CSO] ... which receives almost its sole support through the CRC" in no small part because it promoted democracy by "furnishing the means whereby Mexican Americans' civic consciousness may be expressed" (CRC, Memo, September 6, 1949). CRC members strongly supported the CSO in part because they believed it would, by helping break down the Mexican American community's "suspicion of outsiders," allow the two communities to work more closely together (CRC, Memo, September 6, 1949). Such naïve comments reveal that Jewish community members did not understand the Mexican-origin community very well. Other reasons more likely explained why Mexican Americans remained more isolated than others, including language barriers, constant immigration, and shock remaining from the government-assisted deportations of Mexicans and Mexican Americans during the 1930s, not to mention power imbalances between the Jewish and Mexican communities.

But whatever the reasons, until the CSO the two communities had not had a significant vehicle for political collaboration. Now when members of the Jewish American community like Isaac Pacht, who also chaired the Los Angeles branch of the Council for Equality in Employment—a multiracial organization that fought employment discrimination—wanted to forge alliances with Mexican Americans, he could contact CSO leaders. Pacht did so in 1949 to request their participation on the Council's steering committee (Pacht, Letter to Nava).[9]

At first glance, it seems surprising that members of these two ethnoracial groups would collaborate in the late 1940s and early 1950s. First, the geographic, social, and economic distance between the two was growing, which intuitively makes finding common ground less likely. It seems strange that Jews, who were increasingly integrated and successful, would be interested in joining forces with more marginalized groups like African Americans, Mexican Americans, and others. Second, 1947 was the same year that marked the beginning of the conservative Cold War era, which supposedly stifled meaningful social reform activism. The federal government passed the Taft-Hartley anti-labor act, and states, cities, and counties like California and Los Angeles implemented loyalty oaths, all of which made civil rights activism more difficult. Interracial collaboration, which also was a part of the Communist Party platform, especially appeared dangerous, since even resembling communist programs jeopardized civil rights efforts.[10]

However, the increasing distance between the Mexican American and Jewish American communities and the Cold War are exactly some of the conditions that help explain the CRC's interest in collaborating with the CSO. First, the increasing socio-economic disparity between the two groups in the postwar period ironically impelled Jewish Americans to work to improve conditions for poor Eastside communities like the Mexican-origin population. Because escalating tensions threatened their own safety and security, Jewish Americans hoped to minimize such tensions by helping poorer communities improve their conditions.

Relations between the Jewish and Mexican American communities in East Los Angeles were particularly strained. Mexican Americans saw that while their conditions were not improving, and even perhaps were getting worse, their Jewish neighbors on the Eastside were moving to nicer neighborhoods; even those who stayed benefited from support from the growing—in both size and resources—Jewish community elsewhere in Los Angeles. Increasing social and economic success accompanied the LA Jewish American community's wartime and postwar growth. From 1941 to 1951 the city's Jewish population surged from 130,000 to 315,000 (Vorspan and Gartner 287). This represented a 262% increase in only ten years. Many Jews came to take advantage of wartime opportunities. Many others moved soon after the war to the city of sun, which they first had seen while stationed there in the military. While a greater proportion of earlier migrants settled in the city's poorer and more immigrant eastside, these increasingly middle-class migrants more likely settled in the more affluent—and whiter—West Side. Mexican Americans, on the other hand, were largely confined to ever more isolated Mexican American neighborhoods on the city's eastside.[11]

Increasingly differing class status distanced the two groups from each other. In the schools, for instance, a report observed, "The great barrier to the acceptance of Mexican children by Jewish children is the middle-class bias of the Jewish parents expressed in excessive concern over dirt and disease." This same report by the Chicago-based interracial organization the American Council on Race Relations explained that police action towards the two groups differed and "contribute[d] to the increase of community tension between middle-class Jews and lower-class Mexicans" (American Council on Race Relations 14). Though the report expressed the differences in terms of class, this "class" bias was undoubtedly intertwined with a racial bias, as Jewish Americans were becoming increasingly integrated into American society, and accepted as white, while their fellow Americans increasingly categorized Mexican Americans as brown "others."[12]

Another report by the CSO, surveying the Eastside scene, highlighted this racial and class tension: "The obvious contrast between their neighborhoods and those of other parts of the city bred frustration and bitterness [among Mexican Americans]," the report explained. "These, in turn, found expression in intergroup hostility and scape-goating with particular reference on the Eastside to the adjacent Jewish Community" (CSO/Industrial Areas Foundation).

Additionally, Jewish retailers and landlords were sometimes accused of exploitation by their former Eastside Mexican American neighbors. As Jews across the United States moved up and out socio-economically and geographically in this period, they sometimes retained businesses and rental properties in their former neighborhoods, causing resentment and tensions with the minority communities who remained behind (Conference re the Watts Community Situation).[13]

CRC leaders hoped their support for the CSO would be a key to soothing tensions between Mexicans and Jews on LA's Eastside. They justified Jewish participation by explaining that it "deflects the hostility which exists in that community against the Jews, to constructive social issues of benefit to the Mexican-American and the Jew alike." The CSO could "by its very existence ... prevent race riots such as have happened before in this city." CRC leaders claimed it already had "no doubt prevented serious repercussions which might have otherwise happened on the East Side" (CRC, Memo, September 6, 1949). In this view, the CSO helped not only Mexican Americans but also helped "develop a tremendous amount of understanding among all the groups on the east side" (CRC, Meeting Minutes, February 3, 1950). CRC executive director Herzberg countered a CRC member's protest that the CRC should stop funding the CSO, whose work the member believed to be valuable but not "closely related enough to the activities of the Jewish community," by explaining that its "prophylactic value" was "a relatively cheap investment" for the Jewish community. Preventing "gang fights and similar anti-social acts," Herzberg argued, "was more important than trying to quell such fights after they have begun" (CRC, Meeting Minutes, July 14, 1949). Herzberg's comment about Mexican Americans' supposed proclivity to violence reveals prejudiced assumptions. But it also shows that Jews viewed bridge-building projects as critical for their survival.

Jewish Americans further valued building support from other less successful communities like Mexican Americans (and African Americans) because their own overall increasing wealth and social acceptance did not shield them from discrimination. The persistent discrimination they faced also helps explain Jews' continued interest in collaborative initiatives to fight ongoing inequality. In less than one year—from August 1946 to June 1947—the Bureau of Jewish Economic Problems received 103 complaints from Los Angeles Jews upset with employment discrimination (Jager). Jews faced difficulty securing certain kinds of jobs in the late 1940s and early 1950s, including positions at insurance agencies and banks, and in the finance, mining, petroleum refining, and heavy manufacturing industries. Many private employment agencies refused their applications, arguing they could not place them (Vorspan and Gartner 238–47).[14] Jews also found it hard to break into local politics; early 1950s disputes about the Board of Education were framed in anti-Semitic terms, and many postwar Angelenos willingly received the well-known anti-Semite

Gerald L. K. Smith. The Congregationalist Reverend James W. Fifield and other local anti-Semites' radio sermons reached receptive audiences (Vorspan and Gartner 238–47).[15] The American Automobile Association listed certain hotels as "restricted" from Jews (Kingman). Vandals marked anti-Semitic symbols on Jewish establishments, including painting two swastikas on a Los Angeles temple and six swastikas on stores and walls in one East Los Angeles area, painting crosses on two families' apartment doors, vandalizing a Jewish cemetery in Bell Gardens, and shattering the windows and destroying the Torah of a Jewish community center.[16] Teachers at one eastside junior high school were both "outspokenly anti-Semitic as well as anti-Mexican," according to the American Council on Race Relations, which reported that "the Jewish adolescent discovers that his middle-class status gives him no immunity" (American Council on Race Relations 13). Clearly, Jews' increasing mobility did not mean they were safe, and many sought strategic alliances as a measure of protection.

Civil rights-minded Jewish Americans also hoped that anti-discrimination alliances would help protect them against another postwar danger: red-baiting. The Cold War was a seemingly strange time to begin new collaborative civil rights initiatives, and continue others, because red-baiting made pursuing civil rights activism more dangerous. Extreme red-baiters frequently falsely targeted all civil rights activities as communistic, which threatened to undermine all equality efforts. This was especially true in Los Angeles, a city rumored to have the second largest U.S. Communist Party presence after New York City, as well as Hollywood, long-suspected of harboring communists and other radicals. Los Angeles became the focus of many House Un-American Activities investigations, while California developed the first and one of the strongest state Un-American Activities Committee in the nation, also known as the Tenney Committee after legislator Jack B. Tenney. This committee was particularly active in Los Angeles because of the city's known communist and radical presence. Tenney labeled many Jewish Americans, as well as other minority civil rights activists, communists or fellow travelers, including many groups and individuals with no communist links such as the CRC's Judge Isaac Pacht and the American Jewish Congress.

Reformers like those in the CRC who hoped to maintain their efficacy in the face of mounting anti-communist suspicions responded to such dangers by making their equality initiatives legitimate and all-American. They did so by positioning themselves as anti-communist activists, articulating a middle ground anti-communism which created a space for civil rights. They reclaimed civil rights from the red baiters, carving a space for their approach which they defined as the most American Cold War path because it was an antidote to communism. Their civil rights goals became all-American Cold War imperatives which could help democratically-minded Americans counter both un-American conservatism and radicalism and fight communism most effectively.

Cold War activists labeled as unjust indiscriminate anti-communism which jeopardized "legitimate" civil rights efforts, using language of un-Americanism to shore up their accusations. They charged that indiscriminate anti-communists used the radical label to suppress legitimate struggles to build a more egalitarian society, and thus a better democracy. CRC activists protested that extreme anti-communism targeted civil rights organizations en masse and threatened to entrap all organizations working to extend democracy in the United States by eliminating discrimination, protecting civil rights, and promoting equality of opportunity. The CRC expressed growing opposition to Tenney, for instance, by accusing his committee of undemocratic conduct. The Tenney Committee's false accusation against the American Jewish Congress (he declared it a communist front organization in 1947) was, CRC members explained, "in keeping with [its] unsavory record . . . since its inception—a record replete with instances of the Committee's use of its power to smear liberal American organizations and individuals" (CRC Declaration, 1948). They argued that Tenney's 1949 accusation that Judge Pacht was in the Stalin orbit "aid[ed] and encourage[ed] Communism in our State" (Herzberg, Letter to Pacht). Jewish community activists also claimed that Tenney's downfall would bring a "nation-wide victory for democracy and decency," and joined forces first to defeat his 1952 bid for the 22nd US Congressional District (the San Fernando Valley) and later (1954) his State Senate re-election campaign (Jewish Information Service, *Facts for Action* Report, June 1954).

Their fight against red-baiters who targeted racial equality advocates epitomized Americanism, Cold War CRC activists and their allies in the Jewish community argued. While the efforts of extreme red-baiters to stifle civil rights progress endangered the country, their own efforts to oppose racism helped ensure domestic security by preventing communists from stealing the hearts and minds of minorities. Legislation which unfairly targeted civil rights activists, particularly minorities, was dangerous to democracy, they emphasized. Such legislation would both fail to curb the communist danger and pose new dangers, which would destroy democracy even more surely than communism itself. It threatened to repress legitimate, *democratic*, civil rights activists whose anti-racist platforms resembled communist agendas. Instead, explicitly anti-racist legislation would most effectively defeat communism. All "loyal Americans" who hoped to "combat Communism," CRC allies explained, must help extend civil rights for all Americans, including employment, education, housing, and public accommodation, since communism flourished when minority groups faced discrimination. In these terms, not addressing racial, religious and national origin groups' "just grievances" endangered democracy (Slawson).

Making their own civil rights agenda into tools to fight communism and "increase democracy" meant countering communists as well as extreme anti-communists. Anti-communist activists like those in the CRC marginalized former allies now deemed "unacceptable." Many communities—including labor, African Americans, Jewish Americans, and others—split from within in this way during the early Cold War. In some cases, the anti-communism of the CRC and the organized Jewish community in general was ideological, while in others such agencies asserted that they must protect themselves against being identified with radicalism in order to maintain their effectiveness. The CRC took on "the position as sentinel organization to keep our Jewish community alert to any and all organizations that pose as one thing and are in fact something else," it declared. "Our Jewish community in common with the majority of the American people declares that it is not Communistic or Fascistic and that it is devoted to the American democratic ideals, Constitution and Bill of Rights" (CRC, Press release [undated], 1947).

In one important instance, after much struggle and turmoil from late 1948 until early 1951, the organized Los Angeles Jewish Community expelled one leftist Jewish workers group with about 5,000 Southern California members, the Jewish People's Fraternal Order (JPFO), from its communal structure. The CRC played a key role in this investigation and decision. The CRC explained the danger the JPFO posed and the underlying rationale for this extreme measure. The JPFO's ties to communists and other radical organizations, it emphasized, have "the seeds of great injury to the Jewish Community . . . [in terms of] the state of mind of the general public ['s fear concerning] the recent tenseness between the United States and Russia" (CRC, Meeting minutes, April 2, 1950). Such reasoning led to the JPFO's expulsion.

At the same time, such "all-American" anti-communist activists who recognized the dangers posed by what they viewed as extremes—both red-baiters and communists—looked to other well-reputed groups to shore up their strength and reinforce their anti-communist, civil rights agenda. They decided to build their legitimacy through strategic alliances with acceptable (anti-communist) segments of society and came to believe that they could advance shared goals better together than individually, despite their differences. In this way, the Cold War climate facilitated CRC members' interest in cooperating with Mexican Americans through the CSO.

An urgency to protect themselves from accusations of communism inspired and reinforced the Jewish community's interest in collaborating with the CSO, whose implicit anti-communism it found reassuring. A CSO publicity pamphlet explained the organization's stated anti-communist motivations: "To drive out Communism we must strike at conditions which foster its growth" (CSO, "Across the River"). Bert Corona, a prominent Mexican American reformer at the time, later recalled that limiting communist influence, particularly from the Mexican American "red" members of other Los Angeles organizations, was one of the CSO's reasons for organizing (Garcia 164).[17] Leonard Bloom spoke for many in the Jewish community when he lauded the CSO's efforts to "protect itself from being captured or exploited by Stalinist and Trotskyite elements," and urged the CRC's executive director to support an even "larger and more expensive [CSO] enterprise" in the future (Bloom).

Jews did not always explicitly connect their interest in assisting other minority groups' civil rights struggles to the anti-communist climate, but their organizations' archival records expose this connection even when Jewish activists did not. For example, the CRC filed a Jewish newsletter discussing Jews' interest in Mexican and African American struggles in its "Committee on Communism" folder. The newsletter, published by an agency affiliated with the CRC, explained to Jews why they should be concerned by the condition of Mexican Americans, who were forced into low-paying jobs, subjected to police brutality, "roundup for deportation without due process of law," housing discrimination, and "virtually without representation in government." In short, the newsletter urged, "It is in the interest of Jewish people to support the various Negro and Mexican-American candidates in the Los Angeles area" (Jewish Information Service, *Facts for Action* Newsletter, October 1954). The newsletter's stated reasons that Jews should support civil rights cooperation had nothing to do with communism. But the CRC's choice to file the newsletter with "communism" issues reveals the connection. In this way, Cold War conservatism and the dangers it posed to civil rights activism also facilitated collaborative impulses among activists like those in the CRC who framed their work in moderate, anti-communist terms.

SIGNIFICANCE

The activism of these Los Angeles Jewish Americans groups is significant for several reasons. First, this study reveals the importance of integrating the history of Jewish Americans with that of other minority groups; for they clearly played a role in civil rights struggles in tandem with the other groups. Most literature on racial and ethnic groups in America reinforces contemporary understandings of racial and ethnic categories by considering "racial" groups like Mexican Americans, African Americans, and Asian Americans separately from Jewish Americans, who today are considered as an ethnic or religious minority. The fluidity and complexity of Jewish Americans' status over this earlier time period and the changing nature of their racial categorizations make clear the shortcomings of inflexible understandings of race.

Second, while civil rights stories are often told as stories of East Coast conflicts between whites and African Americans, and sometimes of the Jewish role in the struggle, West Coast civil rights stories expose the role of other groups like Mexican Americans, and the connections between Jewish Americans and these other groups. These western civil rights stories reveal the limitations of focusing exclusively on black/white relations, which cannot fully explain such diverse historical experiences. Moreover, activists in Los Angeles did not merely follow a trickle-down model for civil rights activism established by Southern struggles, but rather simultaneously established their own variety of involvement, which emerged out of the specific multiracial context of Southern California.

Third, these western Jewish activists' ongoing involvement in civil rights efforts exposes important links between the activism of the World War II and early Cold War eras. The bulk of civil rights literature on the late 1940s and early 1950s assumes the Cold War stifled civil rights and laments the ways it limited the earlier more radical possibilities. But this on-the-ground research in Los Angeles reveals that arguing for discontinuity between these periods is far too simplistic. The Cold War shifted the focus of the activism as certain reformers developed an anti-communist approach, but they continued to build upon collaborative efforts from an earlier era as they looked to each other for support and worked to reinforce the legitimacy of their social justice agendas.[18]

Notes

1. For a more detailed discussion of the points discussed in this essay, see my forthcoming book on collaborative civil rights activism in Los Angeles, *Forgotten Coalition: Interracial Civil Rights Activism in World War II and Cold War Los Angeles*.
2. For a discussion of Nazi and Bund activities in Los Angeles, see Scobie 10; and Stephan.
3. For more on the News Research Service, see Eisenberg.
4. For discussions of Hollywood's ties to the CRC and other Jewish organizations in the 1930s, see Gabler; Herman, "Hollywood, Nazism and the Jews, 1933-41"; and Herman, "Jewish Leaders and the Motion Picture Industry." For a broader discussion of Warner Bros.'s involvement in anti-Nazi activity in the 1930s, specifically through several of the films it made in that decade, see Birdwell; and Ross.
5. On Silberberg as a "king maker," see Pitt 10.
6. Some locals estimated that minorities composed forty percent of the city's population by 1950 (Senn). But twenty to thirty percent is probably a more accurate estimate, cf. Vorspan and Gartner 242, and the following information from the census. From 1940 to 1950 the city of LA's population grew from 1,504,277 to 1,970,358 people (United States Bureau of the Census, *Sixteenth Census* 132; United States Bureau of the Census, *Seventeenth Decennial Census* 5–51). The black population increased by over two hundred sixty-eight percent (from 63,774 to 171,209) between 1940 and 1950 (United States Bureau of the Census, *Sixteenth Census* 629 and United States Bureau of the Census, *Seventeenth Decennial Census* 5–100). The Mexican-descent population grew forty-six percent (from 107,680 to 157,067) between 1940 and 1950. The figures for the Mexican-origin population in 1940 and 1950 are estimates, as the census in these periods did not categorize this population separately. The only information we have is from the 1940 census which counted the "Spanish-mother tongue population" in Los Angeles and the 1950 census which counted the "Spanish-surnamed population" in the city. The census numbers are almost certainly undercounts. See United States Bureau of the Census, *Mother Tongue* 34 and United States Bureau of the Census, *Persons of Spanish Surname* 3C-43. The city's Jewish-American population increased by a stunning ninety-two percent from the prewar period to 1948. In 1941 only about 130,000 Jews lived in the city of Los Angeles, and by 1948 there were 250,000 (Vorspan and Gartner 225).
7. Scholarship on other cities and regions suggests that Jews elsewhere also often were in the forefront of cooperative efforts. On events in San Francisco, see Issel. On New York, see Svonkin.
8. The various proposed pieces of state house and senate legislation concerned questions of race in state employment, discrimination in state work, and establishing a California commission on race relations (CRC, Memo of meeting, February 18, 1941).

9. For more on Mexican Americans' perspective, and for more on the CSO, see Bernstein.
10. For more on the Cold War context, see Bernstein.
11. In 1940, Jews lived in both the poor and wealthy areas of LA (twenty-five percent in the poorest areas and twenty-two percent in the wealthiest), but by 1960 they were more prosperous than ever before (Moore 58). For more on Mexican Americans, see Bernstein.
12. For a sample of literature on Jews and whiteness see Goldstein; and Jacobson. On Mexican Americans and "brownness," see, e.g., Foley.
13. On this phenomenon nationwide, for which the literature focuses on relations between African Americans and Jews, see Diner; and Kaufman.
14. For a further discussion of anti-Semitism in postwar Los Angeles see Moore.
15. For more on Fifield and on Smith's visits to Los Angeles, see Sitton 82–92. Also see Leonard.
16. The East Los Angeles area was City Terrace Drive ("Swastika Emblems Like Nazis' Painted on Walls"; "Vandalism Spurs Call for Unity"; and "Vandals Desecrate Synagogue in L.A.; Torah Destroyed").
17. The CSO's anti-communism was less ideological, and less vehement, than the CRC's. For more on this, see Bernstein.
18. For a much more developed discussion of this, see Bernstein.

Works Cited

"6 Southland Folk Indicted as Seditious." *Los Angeles Examiner* Jan. 4, 1944. Schwinn, Herman—Nazi Leader Folder, *Los Angeles Examiner* clippings files. Los Angeles: Regional History Center, Univ. of Southern California.

American Council on Race Relations. "The Problem of Violence: Observations on Race Conflict in Los Angeles." Date undocumented. Carton 6, John Anson Ford Collection. San Marino: Huntington Library.

American Nationalist Party for Nation-Wide Distribution. *A Proclamation.* Sept. 25, 1935. Los Angeles: General Headquarters American Nationalist Party. Reproduced in Carey McWilliams. *It Can Happen Here: Active Anti-Semitism in Los Angeles.* Los Angeles: American League against War and Fascism and Jewish Anti-Nazi League of Southern California, 1935.

Bernstein, Shana. *Forgotten Coalition: Interracial Civil Rights Activism in World War II and Cold War Los Angeles.* New York: Oxford Univ., forthcoming, 2010.

Birdwell, Michael E. *Celluloid Soldiers: Warner Bros.'s Campaign against Nazism.* New York: New York Univ., 1999.

Bloom, Leonard. Memo to Fred Herzberg. Attached to Minutes of the Committee on Agencies, July 14, 1949. Subcommittee: CSO 1949–50, Section AII, Series III. The Jewish Federation Council of Greater Los Angeles' Community Relations Committee Collection. Northridge: Urban Archives Center, Oviatt Library, California State Univ., Northridge.

Conference re the Watts Community Situation. Tues., Feb. 15, 1949. Housing: Watts Community Program (1947–49) Folder, Section 3C, Series III. The Jewish Federation Council of Greater Los Angeles' Community Relations Committee Collection. Northridge: Urban Archives Center, Oviatt Library, California State Univ., Northridge.

Community Relations Council (CRC). Declaration, 1948, Tenney, Jack B. Corr., 1948 Folder, Section 3C, Series III. The Jewish Federation Council of Greater Los Angeles' Community Relations Committee Collection. Northridge: Urban Archives Center, Oviatt Library, California State Univ., Northridge.

———. Meeting Minutes. Aug. 30, 1948. Subcommittees: Agencies—Minutes 1947–50 Folder, Section AII, Series III. The Jewish Federation Council of Greater Los Angeles' Community Relations Committee Collection. Northridge: Urban Archives Center, Oviatt Library, California State U, Northridge.

———. Meeting Minutes. July 14, 1949. Subcommittee: CSO 1949–50 Folder, Section AII, Series III. The Jewish Federation Council of Greater Los Angeles' Community Relations Committee Collection. Northridge: Urban Archives Center, Oviatt Library, California State Univ., Northridge.

———. Meeting Minutes. Feb. 3, 1950. Minutes 1950 Folder, Section AII, Series III. The Jewish Federation Council of Greater Los Angeles' Community Relations

Committee Collection. Northridge: Urban Archives Center, Oviatt Library, California State Univ., Northridge.

———. Meeting Minutes. April 2, 1950. Minutes 1950, Section AII, Series III. The Jewish Federation Council of Greater Los Angeles' Community Relations Committee Collection. Northridge: Urban Archives Center, Oviatt Library, California State Univ., Northridge.

———. Meeting Minutes of Committee on Agencies. Oct. 21, 1949. Minutes 1949 Folder, Section AII, Series III. The Jewish Federation Council of Greater Los Angeles' Community Relations Committee Collection. Northridge: Urban Archives Center, Oviatt Library, California State Univ., Northridge.

———. Meeting Minutes of Public Relations Subcommittee. April 29, 1943. Folder 1—Subcommittees: PR 1943, Box 6, Series II. The Jewish Federation Council of Greater Los Angeles' Community Relations Committee Collection. Northridge: Urban Archives Center, Oviatt Library, California State Univ., Northridge.

———. Meeting Minutes of Subcommittee on CSO. Aug. 31, 1950. Subcommittee: CSO, 1949–50 Folder, Section AII, Series III. The Jewish Federation Council of Greater Los Angeles' Community Relations Committee Collection. Northridge: Urban Archives Center, Oviatt Library, California State Univ., Northridge.

———. Memo. Aug. 13, 1948. Minutes July–Dec. 1948, Section AII, Series III. The Jewish Federation Council of Greater Los Angeles' Community Relations Committee Collection. Northridge: Urban Archives Center, Oviatt Library, California State Univ., Northridge.

———. Memo. Sept. 6, 1949. Memos from Exec Office Staff Nov.–Dec. 1949 Folder, Section AII, Series III. The Jewish Federation Council of Greater Los Angeles' Community Relations Committee Collection. Northridge: Urban Archives Center, Oviatt Library, California State Univ., Northridge.

———. Memo of meeting. Feb. 18, 1941. Folder 29—Legal and Legislative, Feb. 1941, Box 4, Series II. The Jewish Federation Council of Greater Los Angeles' Community Relations Committee Collection. Northridge: Urban Archives Center, Oviatt Library, California State Univ., Northridge.

———. Press Release. 1947. Communism 1947, Section 3C, Series III. The Jewish Federation Council of Greater Los Angeles' Community Relations Committee Collection. Northridge: Urban Archives Center, Oviatt Library, California State Univ., Northridge.

Community Service Organization (CSO). Memo. April 18, 1951. Folder 6, Box 5. Fred Ross Collection. Palo Alto: Department of Special Collections, Stanford Univ.

———. "Across the River," pamphlet, c. 1950. Folder 8, Box 13. Ernesto Galarza Collection. Palo Alto: Department of Special Collections, Stanford Univ.

Community Service Organization (CSO)/Industrial Areas Foundation, Southern California Division. Program, 1949. Folder 11, Box 5. Fred Ross Collection. Palo Alto: Department of Special Collections, Stanford Univ.

Diner, Hasia R. "Between Words and Deeds: Jews and Blacks in America, 1880–1935." *Struggles in the Promised Land: Toward a History of Black-Jewish Relations in the United States.* Ed. Jack Salzman and Cornel West. New York: Oxford Univ., 1997. 87–106.

Eisenberg, Ellen. *The First to Cry Down Injustice? Western Jews and Japanese Removal during World War II.* Lanham, MD: Lexington, 2008.

Foley, Neil. "Becoming Hispanic: Mexican Americans and the Faustian Pact with Whiteness." *Reflexiones 1997: New Directions in Mexican American Studies.* Ed. Neil Foley. Austin: Univ. of Texas, 1998.

Gabler, Neil. *An Empire of their Own: How the Jews Invented Hollywood.* New York: Crown, 1988.

García, Mario T. *Memories of Chicano History: The Life and Narrative of Bert Corona.* Berkeley: Univ. of California, 1994.

Gardner, Joel. *Honorable in All Things: Carey McWilliams.* Oral History Program. Los Angeles: Univ. of California, Los Angeles, 1982.

Goldstein, Eric L. *The Price of Whiteness: Jews, Race, and American Identity.* Princeton: Princeton Univ., 2006.

Guzman, Ralph. Letter asking for CRC help on tax exempt status. Feb. 25, 1950. Subcommittee: CSO 1949–50 Folder, Section AII, Series III. The Jewish Federation Council of Greater Los Angeles' Community Relations Committee Collection. Northridge: Urban Archives Center, Oviatt Library, California State Univ., Northridge.

Herman, Felicia. "Hollywood, Nazism and the Jews, 1933–41." *American Jewish History* 89 (March 2001): 61–89.

———. "Jewish Leaders and the Motion Picture Industry." *California Jews.* Ed. Eva F. Kahn and Marc Dollinger. Boston: Brandeis Univ., 2003. 102–08.

Herzberg, Fred. Letter to CRC members. Feb. 17, 1949. Meeting Notices 1949 Folder, Section AII, Series III. The Jewish Federation Council of Greater Los Angeles' Community Relations Committee Collection. Northridge: Urban Archives Center, Oviatt Library, California State Univ., Northridge.

———. Letter to Isaac Pacht. June 14, 1949. Subcommittee, Special: Tenney Committee 1948–49, AII, Series III. The Jewish Federation Council of Greater Los Angeles' Community Relations Committee Collection. Northridge: Urban Archives Center, Oviatt Library, California State Univ., Northridge.

Issel, William. "Jews and Catholics against Prejudice." *California Jews.* Ed. Eva F. Kahn and Marc Dollinger. Boston: Brandeis Univ., 2003. 123–34.

Jacobson, Matthew Frye. *Whiteness of a Different Color.* Cambridge: Harvard Univ., 1998.

Jager, Marvin (Bureau of Jewish Economic Problems). Letter. June 17, 1947. Discrim. Employment Corresp. 1947–48 Folder, Section 3C, Series III. The Jewish Federation Council of Greater Los Angeles' Community Relations Committee Collection.

Northridge: Urban Archives Center, Oviatt Library, California State Univ., Northridge.

Jewish Information Service. *Facts for Action* Report. June 1954. Folder 10, Box 6, Jewish Secular Material Collection. Los Angeles: Southern California Library for Social Studies and Research.

———. *Facts for Action* Newsletter. Oct. 1954. Communism, Committee On—1954 Folder, Box 68, Series IV. The Jewish Federation Council of Greater Los Angeles' Community Relations Committee Collection. Northridge: Urban Archives Center, Oviatt Library, California State Univ., Northridge.

Kaufman, Jonathan. "Blacks and Jews: The Struggle in the Cities." *Struggles in the Promised Land: Toward a History of Black-Jewish Relations in the United States*. Ed. Jack Salzman and Cornel West. New York: Oxford Univ., 1997. 107–22.

Kingman, Ruth (CFCU). Letter to the SF American Automobile Association. April 30, 1947. Outgoing Correspondence 1947, Box 1. California Federation for Civic Unity Collection. Berkeley: Bancroft Library, Univ. of California, Berkeley.

LeBerthon, Ted. "Ted LeBerthon" (Column). *LA Daily News* June 1, 1943.

Leonard, David J. " 'The Little Fuehrer Invades Los Angeles': The Emergence of a Black-Jewish Coalition after World War II." *American Jewish History* 92 (March 1, 2004): 81–102.

Lewis, Leon. Letter to George Gleason. Nov. 13, 1945. Folder 14—Comm. on Human Relations, LA County: Corresp. July–Dec. 1945, Box 218, Series II. The Jewish Federation Council of Greater Los Angeles' Community Relations Committee Collection. Northridge: Urban Archives Center, Oviatt Library, California State Univ., Northridge.

———. Letter to Walter Hilborn. Feb. 25, 1935. Folder 21—Hilborn, Walter 1935, Box 1, Series I. The Jewish Federation Council of Greater Los Angeles' Community Relations Committee Collection. Northridge: Urban Archives Center, Oviatt Library, California State Univ., Northridge.

———. Letter to Mrs. Mischel. 6 Jan. 1944. Folder 20—Inter-Racial Relations Jan.–June 1944, Box 111, Series II. The Jewish Federation Council of Greater Los Angeles' Community Relations Committee Collection. Northridge: Urban Archives Center, Oviatt Library, California State Univ., Northridge.

———. Letter to Isaac Pacht. Nov. 2, 1933. Folder 31 "Pacht [Judge] Isaac, 1933-37," Box1, Series I. The Jewish Federation Council of Greater Los Angeles' Community Relations Committee Collection. Northridge: Urban Archives Center, Oviatt Library, California State Univ., Northridge.

———. Memorandum. 1934. Folder 15—Lewis, Leon L. [Executive Secretary]: reports, 1933–34, Box 2, Series I. The Jewish Federation Council of Greater Los Angeles' Community Relations Committee Collection. Northridge: Urban Archives Center, Oviatt Library, California State Univ., Northridge.

———. Summary of Operations from June, 1933 to March, 1934. Folder 15—Lewis,

Leon L.: reports, 1933–34, Box 2, Series I. The Jewish Federation Council of Greater Los Angeles' Community Relations Committee Collection. Northridge: Urban Archives Center, Oviatt Library, California State Univ., Northridge.

Los Angeles Jewish Community Council. Letter to members. Feb. 7, 1944. Folder 1—Negroes: National Urban League 1944; 1946, Box 113, Series II. The Jewish Federation Council of Greater Los Angeles' Community Relations Committee Collection. Northridge: Urban Archives Center, Oviatt Library, California State Univ., Northridge.

Moore, Deborah Dash. *To the Golden Cities: Pursuing the American Jewish Dream in Miami and L.A.* New York: Free, 1994.

"More Sedition Cases Seen." *Los Angeles Examiner* Oct. 5, 1943. Schwinn, Herman—Nazi Leader Folder, *LA Examiner* files.

Pacht, Isaac (Chairman of Council for Equality in Employment in LA). Letter to Henry Nava (CSO Chair). 1949 (?). Folder 12, Box 5. Fred Ross Collection. Palo Alto: Department of Special Collections, Stanford Univ.

Pitt, Leonard. Joseph Roos Oral History Interview. Dec. 18, 1979. The Jewish Federation Council of Greater Los Angeles' Community Relations Committee Collection. Northridge: Urban Archives Center, Oviatt Library, California State Univ., Northridge.

Ross, Steven J. "The Politicization of Hollywood before World War II: Anti-Facsism, Anti-Communisim, and Anti-Semitism." *The Jewish Role in American Life: An Annual Review* 5 (2007): 1–23.

Scobie, Ingrid W. "Jack B. Tenney: Molder of Anti-communist Legislation in California, 1940–1949." Diss. Univ. of Wisconsin, 1970.

Senn, Milton A. "A Study of Police Training Programs in Minority Relations." Aug. 7, 1950. Folder 1, Box 5. Fred Ross Collection. Palo Alto: Department of Special Collections, Stanford Univ.

Sherman, G. W. "United They Stand: Another Minority's Fight against Discrimination." Article in *Frontier,* Folder 9—Race: Anti-Mexican Americans, Box 27. American Civil Liberties Union, Southern California. Los Angeles: Department of Special Collections, Charles Young Research Library, Univ. of California, Los Angeles.

Silberberg, Mendel. Letter to Edmund Cooke (the Mayor's office). April 9, 1945 and Oct. 24, 1945. Mayor's Committee for Home Front Unity, LA April–June 1945 Folder 6, Box 13, Series II. The Jewish Federation Council of Greater Los Angeles' Community Relations Committee Collection. Northridge: Urban Archives Center, Oviatt Library, California State Univ., Northridge.

Sitton, Tom. *Los Angeles Transformed: Fletcher Bowron's Urban Reform Revival, 1938–1953.* Albuquerque: Univ. of New Mexico, 2005.

Slawson, John (American Jewish Committee). Letter to American Legion. March 21, 1950. Communism: Jewish—Involvement and Response 1950, 3C, Series III. The Jewish Federation Council of Greater Los Angeles' Community Relations Committee

Collection. Northridge: Urban Archives Center, Oviatt Library, California State Univ., Northridge.

Stephan, Alexander. *"Communazis": FBI Surveillance of German Emigré Writers*. Trans. Jan van Heurck. New Haven: Yale Univ., 2000.

Svonkin, Stuart. *Jews against Prejudice: American Jews and the Fight for Civil Liberties*. New York: Columbia Univ., 1997.

"Swastika Emblems Like Nazis' Painted on Walls." *Los Angeles Times* July 16, 1952. Folder 8, Box 21. Civil Rights Congress Collection. Los Angeles: Southern California Library for Social Studies and Research.

United States Bureau of the Census. *A Report of the Seventeenth Decennial Census of the United States Census of the Population 1950. Vol. II: Characteristics of the Population, Part 5: California*. Washington, DC: US Government Printing Office, 1952.

———. *Sixteenth Census of the United States 1940. Population: Nativity and Percentage of the White Population, Mother Tongue*. Washington, DC: US Government Printing Office, 1943.

———. *Sixteenth Census of the United States 1940. Population, Vol. II: Characteristics of the Population, Part 1: United States Summary and Alabama-District of Columbia*. Washington, DC: US Government Printing Office, 1943.

———. *United States Census of the Population: 1950—Special Reports: Persons of Spanish Surname, Vol. IV, Special Reports Part 3, Chapter C*. Washington, DC: US Government Printing Office, 1953.

"Vandalism Spurs Call for Unity." Unidentified LA newspaper July 24, 1952. Folder 8, Box 21. Civil Rights Congress Collection. Los Angeles: Southern California Library for Social Studies and Research.

"Vandals Desecrate Synagogue in L.A.: Torah Destroyed." *Southwest Jewish Press* Aug. 6, 1954. Vandalism-Violence (Correspondence) 1954 Folder, Box 76A, Series IV. The Jewish Federation Council of Greater Los Angeles' Community Relations Committee Collection. Northridge: Urban Archives Center, Oviatt Library, California State Univ., Northridge.

Vorspan, Max, and Gartner, Lloyd P. *History of the Jews of Los Angeles*. San Marino: Huntington Library, 1970.

The Third Temple: Iranian Jews and the Blessings of Exile—A Personal Memoir

Gina Nahai

Note from the Editors: The following article, written by University of Southern California Lecturer in the Masters of Professional Writing Program and best-selling novelist Gina Nahai, is based on the presentation she delivered for the fifth annual Burton J. Lewis Lecture, sponsored by the Casden Institute for the Study of the Jewish Role in American Life, and delivered on February 18, 2009. This lecture chronicled her personal take on the story of the Los Angeles based Iranian Jewish community through three distinct periods of exile and explored the challenges and transitions this unique community has had to overcome in establishing a new homeland in America. This lecture was particularly significant since it marked the first academic consideration at a major university of the Iranian Jewish community and their numerous contributions to American society since coming to the USA in the aftermath of the Islamic Revolution in 1979.

Due to the relatively recent migration of the Iranian Jewish community, we are very fortunate to have first, second and now third generation oral histories available for study as these immigrants continue to establish themselves in personal, professional and religious arenas—especially in their most dominant venue, Southern California. This community of Jewish immigrants, like the diverse Jewish and non-Jewish communities before it, have followed the well-traveled path to the "American Dream" from new arrivals in a strange but welcoming land to citizens who have woven themselves in their own unique way into the fabric of Southern Californian culture.

Over the last thirty years, the Iranian Jewish community has emerged as one of the nation's most successful, affluent and best-educated ethnic groups. Due to its passionate concern for Israel and strong traditional Jewish values, this community has also made significant cultural and philanthropic contributions to a wide range of Jewish causes. The national interest that Professor Nahai's lecture generated has served as a foundation for the academic exploration of the Iranian Jewish community in America for many institutions of higher learning across the country and in Israel.

Because Prof. Nahai thinks and writes primarily as a creative artist, as is seen in her many avidly read novels, chronicling the Iranian Jewish experience in Southern California, her lecture does not follow the normal, more prosaic conventions of academic writing. Prof. Nahai is, first and foremost, a storyteller and in this essay she allows the more personal aspects of her experience, leaving one home in order to find another, to come to the forefront. Yet if she speaks in highly personal terms about her own life-experience, one may see in this much more: that, in essence, the struggle of a group to find their way from Iran to Los Angeles is really the aggregation of many individual narratives that must be listened to carefully and sympathetically, a point well made by Marsha Kinder elsewhere in this volume. Thus, in giving voice to her own immigrant experience, Prof. Nahai is also able to speak on behalf of her community.

Ask me today what I remember of my life in Iran, and I will say, "very little." That's true, but perhaps misleading: I can indeed recall a great deal of Iran and its people, of its physical space and landscape, its natural rhythms of life and social fabric. I can easily summon up the sounds and scents, the colors and cadences that surrounded me there in my childhood and early youth. What I *can't* recollect—what seems to have fallen into a well so deep, I haven't managed to find the bottom of it in thirty years of looking back, is me *in* that life.

It's like I'm watching a movie I've made about my past, only without a trace of me in it.

*****

I left Iran in the summer of 1974. That was five years before the fall of the Shah, in the heyday of his rule and the golden age of Jewish history in Iran. Unlike the vast majority of their fellow Iranian Jews, my parents had long wanted to live in the United States. But they never thought, as they planned our move to Los Angeles and even for the first few years of our life here, that our departure from Iran would be as absolute and as lasting as it proved to be. The Jewish people of Iran had existed on the land since before there was an Iran or a Persian Empire; their national and religious identities had been formed and cultivated as one—each as ingrained as the other. One scorching August day in Tehran, we hugged our grandparents and aunts and uncles, kissed the servants, shook hands with the neighbors, and promised we would be back to see them all very soon. I left my room, my bed, my books of fairy tales just as they had always been—just as I believed I would find them again upon my next visit. I left my blue-eyed plastic dolls asleep in the bottom drawer of my yellow dresser, left the silver gun and brown leather holster I used to play cowboys and Indians with my cousin, left the white paper daisies and the starched silk handkerchiefs I had learned to make that summer. I left them thinking they would be there, waiting, untouched and undisturbed, until I returned.

For years after the revolution, I dreamt that I had returned to that house. I would walk through its narrow hallways, up the long, stone and wood staircase, through door after door until I came upon my bedroom and went inside. My bed was unmade, but empty. The sheets had turned yellow; the windows were shaded with dust; the wood of my yellow dresser turned to powder at the touch. I had fallen asleep, I realized, and woken up a thousand years later.

What do you gain, and lose, when you leave a homeland behind?

*****

To be erased from the pages of one's own past. To be denied a chance to return, a right to belong. To have the doors close on you so irrevocably, you can neither imagine nor mentally place yourself on the inside any more. This is the price that I, and so many of my compatriots, paid for leaving. It's not a cheap bargain, nor is it unique to me, or my to fellow Iranian Jews, but it's one I believe well worth making.

*****

In the thirty years since they came to settle in Los Angeles, Iranian Jews have penetrated and often excelled in just about every facet of American society. Our first generation, people now in their seventies and eighties, have managed not only to survive the shock of dislocation, but to maneuver with uncanny skill an alien culture with unfamiliar practices in everything from personal values to commerce and industry and trade. Our second generation, those in their forties and fifties, have been leaders in many a chosen field—in the arts and medicine, in technology and theology. Our children have been admitted to the most competitive schools and universities, and graduated with honors.

Along the way, we have maintained the best of the old country's cultural and social values—a sense of family, of loyalty, of friendship; an awareness of the importance of learning, an ambition and a work ethic and a unique resilience, an ability to adapt and accept, to bend, as we say in Persian, instead of breaking, that was the secret of our survival in Iran and that has enabled us to move forward so effectively in America. We have established and maintained synagogues and cultural centers, schools and youth groups and elderly care facilities that have grown in strength and far-reaching influence with every passing year. We have been staunch and effective supporters of the state of Israel, and of Jewish people in need everywhere else.

And we have shed much of the less commendable attributes of the traditional society from which we came. Today, we are more tolerant of diversity, more accepting of defiance. We are more humble, less entitled, more introspective, less chauvinistic.

We have done all this in spite of a not-always welcoming or hospitable host country. In spite of the negative image of all Iranians created and cultivated by the mullahs and their posse. In spite of the hostage crisis, the Hezbollah, September 11th. In spite of the elderly Ashkenazi gentlemen who dislike all Iranian Jews just because some of them have the unfortunate habit of speaking only Persian even in the company of Americans, and the little old Jewish ladies who blame everything from global warming to the common cold on the gaudy eyesores with flat roofs and too many columns that a handful of Iranians have built in Beverly Hills.

We thrived because we had set up house in a country that, for all its spotty record of the treatment of minorities, including Jews, opened its arms to us in 1979 and thereafter, and gave us all the rights, all the opportunities, all the chances we could have asked for and more. We did it with the help of American

Jewish institutions—the Hebrew Immigrant Aid Society (HAIS), the Jewish Federation, Chabad, the Jewish Educational charity ORT, and others—with the aid of American laws and constitutional guarantees. With the good will and generosity of American citizens.

And perhaps, too, we succeeded because we knew about this—living elsewhere, starting again, reinventing ourselves. Because we had done it twice already over the course of our 2,500-year history.

The first time was when Nebuchadnezzar destroyed the first temple and brought the Jews as slaves into the area that, seventy years later, would become the Persian Empire. When the first Persian emperor, Cyrus the Great, freed the slaves and allowed Jews to return to their homeland and rebuild their temple, about half of them took a chance and stayed in Persia. In a foreign land with alien customs and nothing but their own mental resources, yesterday's slaves became tomorrow's soldiers and scientists, its poets and philosophers, teachers and inventors.

And we did it again, in the six decades between the Constitutional Revolution of 1917 and the fall of the Shah in 1979. Released from the ghettoes after seven centuries of poverty and oppression, having had little or no access to an education, having been considered, in spite of their presence on the land for two and a half millennia, "foreigners," the Jews of Iran rose from the ashes of tyranny in the name of Islam to the highest social, cultural, and economic ranks in the country's history.

We know about survival, about endurance and sacrifice, about being strangers in our homeland and making a home in strange lands.

What do you gain, and lose, when you become an outsider on every soil?

*****

Once, years ago when my oldest son was a toddler, I sat in a circle among a group of new mothers at a Jewish day school on LA's west side. The school was only minutes away from where I lived, and the parent group was made up of neighborhood families. For one hour each week, while our children "socialized" on the rug next to us, we, the mothers, were supposed to get to know each other, exchange vital information on breast-feeding and thumb-sucking and diapers, and establish a bond that would, well-meaning school administrators hoped, carry us all through the next eighteen years of our children's Jewish education.

Because this was the first meeting for our group, the pre-school teacher assigned to us made a point of asking each mother to introduce herself and—this being Southern California—"share" some thoughts and feelings about parenthood. I don't remember what I said, except perhaps that I found the entire experience well above my pay-grade, and I don't remember what anyone else said either, except for the last woman—an American Jew who lived three blocks away from me, I found out that day, and had two children under the age of six. She had short brown hair and a dark, angry frown, and she looked older than everyone else in the group. She didn't have time to stand on ceremony so she got right to the point and told us all that her life was a living hell: she was suffering from Multiple Sclerosis and couldn't work, and she had lost both her parents the previous year and her husband had just upped and left her because he "wanted to be happy again" and didn't feel like hanging around a sick woman in mourning, he'd found himself a new love and moved to Phoenix, so that she—my neighbor—was all alone with the kids (and here, she broke down and started to sob) with no help and no money to hire any, she might actually lose the house and sometimes, she couldn't even take care of the children's physical needs, all she could do was lie in bed and listen to them cry.

The woman said all this in one breath, and when she was done, she just looked down at her hands while the rest of the group sat in a stunned silence for a minute or so, until the teacher cleared her throat and, to my astonishment, moved right ahead with the hour's agenda which—this being Southern California—consisted of a discussion of the virtues of fruit juice versus breast milk. Troubled by her seemingly insensitive reaction to what we had just witnessed, I opened my mouth to object, but before I could say anything I saw that the other mothers welcomed the new topic of discourse all too warmly, that they were relieved and grateful to change the subject away from someone's tragic circumstance to their own pressing juice-issues, and then I heard a woman next to me lean over and whisper to the person on her right that she couldn't believe some people's selfishness, bringing their private troubles into the "group" and trying to make it "all about them"—this was supposed to be a relaxing time for busy mothers like herself, not talk therapy for somebody with a straying husband.

So I listened to the others speak, and after a while even the woman with the straying husband began to talk about the virtues of cranberry versus apple juice, but right when the teacher invited us all to take our children into our lap and sing some asinine "goodbye, goodbye, see you next time" rhyme, I spoke up: given the one mother's current difficulties, I suggested, perhaps we should all step up and offer whatever help we could give with child care or baby-sitting. Before the whole group, I told the woman I would be happy to go to her house or to bring her children to mine any time she felt ill or needed a break; they could stay as long as they wanted and they would be well fed and cared for and it would be a pleasure, really, no trouble at all; we were neighbors and fellow parents and here's my phone number, please call me any time.

She looked at me impassively, saying nothing.

The teacher, though, suddenly found her Jewish conscience and chimed in, announcing this was a great idea, Mitzvah and *tikkun olam* and what not, and all of a sudden the sick woman had warmed to the idea and started taking down names and phone numbers, expressing gratitude and relief to each mother as she did so. One by one, she went around the circle and took down everyone's information, but when she reached me, she just skipped to the next person.

That should have been my cue. I should have known she wasn't interested in my help, but I was naïve and clueless, still operating on the assumption that human beings are put on this earth in order to reach out to one another, create lasting bonds—that sort of thing. So I interrupted the woman and said, "Wait, you don't have my number yet."

There was a pall. Everyone stared at me. I was the only Iranian in the group. The woman, I realized too late, did not like Iranians; she probably didn't like the idea of having one as a neighbor. It didn't matter that we were all Jews, that I had shown more concern for her than anyone else had. That I spoke English fluently, looked like everyone else.

"No," she said. "Not *you*. I don't want *your* number."

To set up house in a country at war with your own. To be ashamed for your compatriots—at once a victim of, and blamed for, their actions. To have your neighbors dislike you for being among them, to be told to "go home" by strangers in a post-office line, a restaurant, a public library. To have rich American women yelling obscenities at you outside expensive Beverly Hills department stores because "you've come here and driven all the prices up."

To make many a futile attempt at reaching out to "the natives" at your school or university, to undertake many a vain effort to feel accepted as "one of us" by your colleagues, to fall into many a hopeless cycle of self-doubt and soul-searching every time you try, and fail, to establish a friendship with the families of your children's friends, to push past that line beyond which you are not allowed—a set of friendly but indifferent eyes, a series of polite but noncommittal remarks that serve as notice that you are viewed and understood according to a different set of standards—not before the law, but by the people. This, too, is the collective burden of immigrant populations everywhere.

And yet.

*****

Just the other day my younger son, a teenager, asked me about my childhood and early youth. Who were your friends, he wanted to know. Where are they now? What was your house like in Iran? What happened to your school? What music did you listen to? What became of all those strange aunts and uncles you write about in your books?

Every one of my three children has, at one time or another, asked these questions. They ask because they can sense the void—the physical absence of things and people, the dark and empty places in my memory, the lack of that elusive but all too significant sense of ownership, of belonging and connectedness—that distinguishes me from their friends' parents.

I didn't have many friends in elementary school because I was a Jew in a Muslim country, the only Jewish kid in my class and one of the very few in the school. My mother, who had suffered much discrimination and heard many more horror stories, distrusted Muslim families with her children. I didn't have many friends in boarding school in Europe because I couldn't adapt quickly enough to the other girls' more adventurous, more independent attitude. I was homesick and lost and lonely most of the time, struggling to learn the ways of European and American teenage girls, afraid to imitate them and in the process, lose my more traditional standards. I didn't have many friends in the first couple of years after I moved to LA because I was still a rarity, most people didn't even know where Iran was on the map and when they found out, they thought it alien and inferior.

That's the difficult part of the story I have to tell my children.

The happy part is that I started making friends, learning what music I was listening to, living in places that still exist, that I can go back and revisit, only after the Islamic Revolution forced the better part of the Iranian Jewish community toward the United States. It was a community of refugees, yes, but one that had found safe harbor and that quickly found its sea legs; that was able to, and allowed, to retain a basic sense of identity, the tribal mentality that accounts for the enduring bond and the strong sense of belonging among its members.

It is to the great credit of this country and its laws and founding principles, and also the majority of its tolerant, generous population that we have managed to make a home in what could easily have been permanent exile. Exile implies an alone-ness, a disconnectedness, a sense of being unmoored and unsettled that I and, I dare say, most other Iranian Jews, have not experienced in the United States for at least two decades. It implies an abiding sense of loss, a constant longing to return—to another time, or another place—that I doubt many of us have experienced except in the early days of the revolution. It is to the credit of the Iranian immigrant community, the strength and endurance of the Persian culture, the resilience and flexibility of most Iranian Jews, that we have been able to "become" American without letting go of, or denying, or even hiding from the outside, so much of our old selves.

To be able to assert, with complete honesty and in spite of the hardships you have encountered, that being forced out of your ancestral home was the best thing that could have happened to you and your people; that what seemed like an irrevocable loss at the time, has proven to be a blessing many times over—*this,* I believe, is the great paradox, the uncommon triumph of the Iranian Jewish experience in America.

But to say that this ability to keep one foot on each side of the divide has been a source of strength for our community, to say that America's embracing of multiculturalism and Iranian Jews' insistence on maintaining their distinct identity have yielded precious gains for both sides, is not to deny the many cultural risks that can inhibit the ideal of forming a truly cohesive society, nor does this overlook the many painful obstacles that must be faced, in particular, by our youth.

*****

"I have too little in common with my Iranian-born family and too many differences with the American kids I grew up with," many young people have told me. "I don't feel I belong with either group. I wish my parents had either raised me in Iran or, if they wanted to live in America, integrated more fully and raised me like a *real* American."

To be raised like a real American, I am told by many "native" Jews who admit they dislike Iranians, would seem to replicate the practices of Ashkenazi communities who fled Europe in the earlier part of the last century.

"My parents never spoke Yiddish (or German, or whatever their native tongue had been) at home," those "natives" insist, perhaps recalling a transition—from European Ashkenazi to "just plain American"—that wasn't as seamless as their memory suggests.

"Their English wasn't good, but they wanted to learn, and wanted us to speak like Americans. They barely even spoke of the old country, or the Holocaust, because they wanted their children to feel like everyone else."

I suspect that these parents, in their attempt to shield their offspring from the sting of exile, neglect to mention the troubles that *they* encountered on the road to becoming American; that they weren't really so different from the generation of Iranian Jews that is now being blamed by the children of that older wave of immigrants. But I also believe that Iranian Jews treasure their Persian past and all its cultural vestiges in a way that is unique among Jewish-American populations.

Our past. Our stories. Our inherited and acquired memories. This is what we Iranian Jews have given our young people when we cling to our separate identity. Is that a gift, or a burden? A sacrifice on our part, or a selfish act?

Have we, in an attempt to preserve for them a rich cultural heritage, installed in our children a hybrid sense of self? Have we asked too much of them, built too many fences around them, condemned them to being a small minority within an already small minority? Have we ensured that they will come up against the same invisible wall that their parents know so well and thus reinforced the line that separates real Americans from perpetual immigrants? Is that why so many children of Iranian Jewish heritage travel in packs, befriend mostly each other, alienate or are alienated from their all-American peers? Is this whey most mixed marriages—between Iranians and Jews from other cultures—fail? Then again, how much integration is too much?

What do you gain, and lose, when you refuse to let go of the country you've left behind?

*****

I suspect that the thirty years of darkness, the decades during which we have not been able to return to Iran or to take our children to see the place—all the physical traces of our past that vanished the moment we escaped to the West but that we continue to safeguard, that we try so hard to preserve in that amorphous, elusive and intangible form we refer to as "culture"—will forever stand like an emotional moat separating each one of our successive generations.

My little sister, all fair skin and freckles, speaking French like a native but not a word of English, leaving her school, her friends, her room full of Barbies. At home, she is cautioned to be quiet in class, act in a deferential manner toward her teachers, be respectful of her peers. In school, she's shunned by the other kids because she's not "cool." Being cool, she learns, means being overly confident, irreverent, disdainful of good manners and social graces. She has a choice—to succeed socially and fail her family, or to be an outcast all through middle and high-school in order to maintain the values her culture has taught her.

My father, thirty-two years old with three young daughters, leaving the house that was his father's pride and joy, putting his faith in a country that, if one were to believe the nay-sayers, corrupts the most pious of women and turns every teenage girl into a foul-mouthed, guitar playing, cigarette-smoking drug-addict. In Iran, he has learned to do business on the assumption that a person's word means something, that deals are made *khoda vakili*—with God as your attorney. In America, he finds he can't buy a piece of gum without having a lawyer look at the fine print on the packet, but that he can spend thousands of dollars, buy a car, a house, anything he wants, without having the money to pay for it. He buys on credit, but isn't able to pay the debt. He's ashamed of his own failure, feels he's losing ground as the head of the family, so he hides his troubles and borrows more.

My mother's mother, married at age twelve, having borne ten children, lost two and raised eight, became the rock of her family and the *bozorg*—doyenne—of her community. She knew every cop and street kid and shop owner in her Tehran neighborhood, but she's never exchanged a word with the people who live next door to her in LA, they just come and go and pretend they haven't seen her if they happen to cross paths. She wants to talk to her children but they're always too busy; tries to talk to the grandkids but they don't understand her broken, halting English.

There is, I have learned, such a thing as emotional exile. The longer we, of the old country, cling to that which provides for us a sense of security, the more we undermine our children's sense of belonging—to us, or to this country, to history, or to the future.

How many more times, I wonder, will I stare at the pictures of people I know I once knew, the places I know I have been to but of which I have no memory—before I give up on the effort to reclaim my past? How many times will I examine the fading images my parents own of what they claim is me as a child, try to find in them a spark of recognition, a sliver of a memory, before I can let go of what is no longer mine?

How do I relay, my best intentions notwithstanding, to my children, the sadness of Friday morning *azzans*—prayer calls—in Iran, the color of Tehran's sky at night, the feel of the cold air on my face on a snowy school morning? How do I explain to them the difference between my own idea of happiness, of contentment and satisfaction, my own measure of realistic expectations and pragmatic aspirations—what I was taught as a child, and what they, my American children, have learned and lived in this very different home?

"Life is hard; get used to it." "Success means fulfilling one's responsibility to the family and the community; happiness has nothing to do with it."

We may each be only two or three decades apart—my parents, my children, and me, but in many ways—ways that matter—we are of different worlds. The same belief system and values that saved my parents and me from feeling alienated and lost in America, the same awareness of history and upholding of tradition that has given our children a certain grounding and an impetus to succeed—the very precious freedom to maintain in the West our Eastern ways of life—has driven a deep and painful gash into the soul of our young. We of the eternal sense of estrangement, heirs to the peripatetic tenants of the destroyed First Temple—*we* may be content with belonging only to ourselves, but we cannot expect the same of children born on solid ground. They have a right to feel they belong to this country and that it, in turn, belongs to them.

*****

Up until the very end, when the Shah left and his army folded, most Iranian Jews couldn't fathom leaving Iran for good. Like Iraqi Jews before us, like Egyptian and Syrian Jews, like Austrian and German and French Jews—like all the Jews who believed they belonged to a country and that it belonged to them, who stayed too long or left on an hour's notice—we invested our love, goodwill, the energy and ability of our young in Iran, and then we were betrayed.

Small wonder, then, that so many of us have chosen, in America, the safety and certainty of a rather narrow, often insular horizon. Family, God, Religion. We think of achievement in individual terms—for ourselves and our children, for Israel, for other Jews. We vote our pocketbooks, Israel and, to a lesser degree, Iran. We measure success mostly in financial terms, aspire more toward uniformity than originality. Instead of encouraging our children to explore and discover their own potential, we raise them to become *us*—only with more trappings of success. Instead of using our resources to search for new frontiers, we do our best to be like everyone else, only better. We socialize with each other and travel with each other, worship together, read the same books. We even go to group therapy with each other.

We search for fulfillment and a sense of purpose—we, who fled Iran in part because it insisted on keeping the women covered according to Muslim law—by becoming more religious, covering our hair and body according to Jewish law, building bigger fences around ourselves and our community.

Only we've opted, you see, to live in the United States. Our children are American citizens. Whatever price we have paid for leaving Iran, whatever gains or losses we have made in the past thirty years, we are, today, at a turning point in our long and eventful story—the moment when a people transitions from being driven by outside events to being able to drive them.

Yes, we have adjusted well, settled in, become more or less integrated.

Yes, we have cared for the less fortunate among ourselves and certainly for the state and the people of Israel. Yes, we realize that we're never going back, that we are bound to this land because we have buried our dead in it and borne our children on it.

Now what?

What are we going to do, not for ourselves or even for Israel, but for this country we've made our home? What are we going to build, given all our resources, that will outlast our own immediate experience and give back to America as it has given us? How are we going to teach our children that they owe this country at least as much as it has given *them*, that they have a duty to create something of value not just *in* America but *for* America?

It's an unsettling question, I know: We are, after all, a people accustomed to being strangers in our own land, to devoting our resources first to fight the battle at hand and then, should we be so lucky, to prepare for the calamity we know is just around the corner. We remain a small community; we have a responsibility to each other and to other Jews.

But we're also a people capable of giving (and I don't mean only financially) to more than one cause. It would be the paucity of our faith, not a lack of resources, that would make us hesitant to commit to this country as we have to Israel, as we did to Iran.

There was a time, not so long ago, when entire Jewish families saved and sacrificed in the ghettoes of Iran, only so they could send just *one* of their own to the West. They did this not just in pursuit of wealth, but more so in hopes that the chosen one would learn, and bring back with them, the much larger horizons, the different ways of thinking, the more revolutionary world view, than what we had access to in Iran.

That worldview was worth something then, and it is still worth something today. It's what made us fall in love with the *idea* of America even before we thought we might end up living in this accommodating country. It's valuable not because it affirms and strengthens what we already believe, but because it challenges long-held assumptions, gives the individual permission to think differently from the tribe, to act differently, to have different goals without being considered strange, or bizarre, or rebellious.

Thirty years after their forced departure from home, Iranian Jews must have the courage, perhaps the confidence, to uphold that greatest of American values, the principle upon which the first great Persian emperor, Cyrus the Great founded his empire: tolerance of the *other*.

So that, a hundred years from now when our children's children look at *our* pictures the way we look at our parents' images of a time and a place that no longer really exists, they can say about us that we took a chance on this country and won, that we put our faith in history not repeating itself this *one* time, bet that we would not have to leave, or be driven away, from this *one* land. That, without taking away from ourselves or Israel, we managed to build here a third temple that will stand for another 3000 years.

Jewish Homegrown History:
In the Golden State and Beyond

Marsha Kinder

BUILDING A TRANSMEDIA NETWORK

In Spring 2006, my colleague Rosemary Comella and I met with Bill Deverell to choose a topic for a collaborative project involving our two research groups—the Huntington-USC Institute on California and the West directed by Deverell, and the Labyrinth Research Initiative on Database Narrative and Digital Scholarship, which I founded at USC in 1997 and where Comella has worked as a creative director since 1999.[1] We agreed that whatever subject we chose, the project would draw on the archival resources of the Huntington Library and of USC Libraries' Special Collections and would leverage Labyrinth's ten years of experience producing archival cultural histories as large-scale museum installations, drawing on Comella's expertise as a multimedia artist.

The topic we chose was a cultural history of Jews in California, which would be presented to the general public in three different modes: as an on-line multimedia archive, a traveling museum installation, and a print-anthology edited by Deverell (the volume in which this essay appears). Together these public presentations would comprise (what we at Labyrinth call) a "transmedia network," the use of multiple media to create a series of networked public spaces that enable participants to engage with the same material in different ways. By employing different media, the project focuses the attention of users on the content, where it belongs.

With seed money from USC's Casden Institute for the Study of the Jewish Role in American Life, we began the research, commissioned an extensive bibliography by Jewish Studies scholar Karen Wilson, and broadened our collaborative base to include other partners. With grants from the Haas, Righteous Persons, and NEH Foundations and from the Friends of Tel Aviv University, we expanded the original concept to make it a national project. Although we remained committed to starting with California as originally planned, our ultimate goal is to show how this new information about Jews in the West might alter our broader understanding of Jews in America—a shift that would be best understood if our project had a national scope.

But how could we possibly "cover" such a broad field? We realized that, like many of Labyrinth's previous installations, this project would be an open-ended database narrative that would create a productive dialogue between what is already known about Jewish cultural history and new information contributed by the general public. We assembled an Advisory Board of historians, Jewish studies scholars, archivists, documentary filmmakers, and museum curators who have assisted us in identifying key issues and contributed passages from their own works that have helped shape the "scaffolding" of published history we are building. Thus, our expanding project and its dialogic history can be based on a system of social networking that relies on contributions not only from the general public but also from scholars, filmmakers and other cultural institutions.

Having named our project, *Jewish Homegrown History: Immigration, Identity, Intermarriage*, we are committed to showing how the concept of the Jewish homeland has continued to grow, as Jewish immigrants have come to America from different parts of the world in different eras and have migrated to and settled within different locations across the United States, where they have interacted with other communities. We decided to explore this expanding concept of the Jewish homeland through three inter-related sub-themes: *Immigration & Migration*, the negotiation of loyalties both to the old country and to the new locations of settlement within the USA; *Identity & Cultural Contributions*, the negotiation of conflicts that arise from identifying both as an American and as a Jew and from assessing what distinctive contributions the Jewish community has made to American culture; and *Intermarriage & Other Alliances*, the negotiation of complex relations, both alliances and estrangements, with other ethnic groups in America, particularly those encountered within the local site of settlement.

During the early period of production, several people from within the Jewish community questioned our inclusion of "intermarriage" as one of the principal three subthemes. We explained that we were using this term not only literally but also in the broader sense of addressing the alliances and oppositions between Jews and other groups, and were showing how this issue was interwoven with the other two subthemes of identity and immigration. Still, several religious people warned us it was too controversial, while other secular Jews (especially from the Bay Area) claimed that intermarriage was now so widely accepted that it did not need to be emphasized. What was clear from these discussions was the emotional heat this issue still generates, which is one of the reasons we decided to include it. We were also convinced by the following statement by Jonathan Sarna (one of our Advisory Board members) in his book on American Judaism:

> Freedom, the same quality that made America so alluring for persecuted faiths, also brought with it the freedom to make religious choice: to modernize Judaism, to assimilate, to intermarry, to convert. American Jews, as a result, have never been able to assume that their future as Jews is guaranteed. Each generation has had to wrestle anew with the question of whether its own children and grandchildren would remain Jewish, whether Judaism as a living faith would end and carry on as ancestral memory alone. The history of American Judaism, as I have come to understand it, is in many ways a response to this haunting fear.... But the story of American Judaism recounted in this book is not just a stereotypical tale of "linear descent," of people who start off Orthodox and end up intermarrying. It is, instead, a much more dynamic story of people struggling to be Americans and Jews, a story of people who lose their faith and a story of people who regain their faith, a story of assimilation, to be sure, but also a story of revitalization (xiii–xiv).

The ongoing nature of this story and its emphasis on non-linear spatial exploration make it particularly well suited to an open-ended database narrative (Labyrinth's signature genre), which is being presented both as an on-line multimedia archive that will continue to grow as people contribute their own family histories, and as an interactive museum installation that will expand in scope as it travels across the nation.

The on-line archive will be publicly launched in 2010; and the traveling installation is scheduled to open in three California venues in 2010–2011: the Skirball Cultural Center in Los Angeles (September 2010–January 2011), the New Americans Museum in San Diego (January–April 2011), and the Judah L. Magnes Museum in Berkeley (May–September 2011). The installation will then travel eastward to Philadelphia, where it will open at the National

Museum of American Jewish History in 2012, as well as in New York and other cities to be determined. Given that this project is still in production, this essay will describe its development and some of the issues it has raised along the way, starting with our choice of database narrative.

DATABASE NARRATIVE AND THE PARADOX AT THE HEART OF COLLECTING

Although Labyrinth's previous cultural histories differ in content, they are all "database narratives," a structure that reveals the process by which certain narrative fragments—characters, events, settings, objects—are chosen from an underlying database and recombined to make stories. Operative in all languages and all narratives (both history and fiction), these interwoven processes of selection and combination are performed both by authors and users, but frequently they remain hidden. By deliberately exposing these dual processes, database narrative diffuses the force of master narratives, which can no longer be seen as merely *natural* or, even more simply, *the truth*, because users are reminded that alternative versions of the story and new combinations of the components are always possible. Instead of master narratives, what emerges is a more open narrative field full of possibilities, which is in turn fueled by an underlying database that continues to grow.

Despite all the hype in the early 1990s about the obsolescence of narrative and its replacement by spatial exploration and database structures, narrative has remained a crucial organizational principle in the digital age. For narrative is a cognitive mode found in every human society. In the broad cognitive sense, narrative contextualizes the meaning of sensory perceptions: it maps the world and our own position within it. That is why narratives are constantly under reconstruction and must remain open-ended—whether they are the public histories of a nation or people, or the personal stories of individuals and their families—since they must continually account for the influx of new data in their latest remix. As historian Hayden White puts it: "Far from being one code among many that a culture may utilize for endowing experience with meaning, narrative is a metacode, a human universal on the basis of which transcultural messages about the nature of a shared reality can be transmitted" (1).

Instead of defining database and narrative as an opposition (as several new media theorists do),[2] at Labyrinth we see them working together. By combining database (a dominant form in contemporary digital discourse whose politics tend to be discounted or disavowed) with narrative (the traditional form it supposedly displaces whose ideological baggage is well known), the database narrative actually exposes the ideological underpinnings of both. Like cultural historian Diana Taylor, we believe that every database or archive is designed for a particular kind of knowledge production and comes with specific (if not necessarily explicitly stated) goals; and the decision of which items to include or exclude, what categories to use as structuring principles, and what metadata to collect (or exclude) for later retrieval—all of these decisions serve ideological ends. In our works, we frequently visualize the database structure so that the interface design exposes this process of knowledge production, which is precisely what happens in *Jewish Homegrown History*.

Database narrative raises an interesting paradox. On the one hand, it ruptures the narrative's illusion of wholeness by revealing the gaps (through its lack of closure) and by showing what is omitted (the other fragments not chosen). Yet by exposing the underlying database, it potentially introduces another pleasurable illusion of wholeness—as if all of the possibilities really were contained in the database. Acknowledging this paradox, French theorist Gilles Deleuze sees it as a reason for exposing the gaps:

> But sometimes, on the contrary, it is necessary to make holes, to introduce voids and white spaces, to rarify the image, by suppressing many things that have been added to make us believe that we were seeing everything. It is necessary to make a division or make emptiness in order to find the whole again (21).

In database narrative it is possible to emphasize either side of the paradox—the gaps or the illusion of wholeness. In our work at Labyrinth, we choose to emphasize the gaps because we consider this epistemological tension a great strength of database narrative.

A similar paradox lies at the heart of collecting, an activity featured in all database narratives. On the one hand, collectors dream of making their collection "complete," of gaining total knowledge of their subject. This is a dream one can aspire to but never really attain—because one never knows what new (or old) data will emerge in the future. On the other hand, rarity is what makes the collectible valuable, and rarity depends on loss—the loss of most of the other objects in this category. If the relic were commonplace and ubiquitous, then one might be less inclined to collect it.

Every collector (like every author of database narrative) is faced with the question: should I emphasize the illusion of wholeness or the gaps. This question is especially pivotal in a field like Jewish Studies, where some enemy ideologues challenge the existence of material evidence for the Holocaust and even question whether it actually happened. Thus, we can understand the drive to create a comprehensive archive that promises to preserve total knowledge of what happened, as is the goal of the Shoah Foundation Institute for Visual History and Education, for example, where it is not only a matter of producing and collecting thousands of extensive interviews with survivors but also conducting them in multiple languages. We find the opposite tendency in Alain Resnais's powerful thirty-minute documentary on the Holocaust, *Night and Fog* (*Nuit et brouillard*, 1955), which, despite its display of ghastly footage of the death camps, insists in a poetic voice-over that we can never fully know what it was like to have been there: "No description, no picture can restore their true dimension: endless, uninterrupted fear. . . . Of this brick dormitory, of these threatened sleepers, we can only show you the shell, the shadow." Given that collecting material evidence is crucial in both cases and for the same goal of preventing the repetition of genocide, then, we may ask, what is at stake in the choice between striving for total knowledge versus calling attention to the gaps?

By emphasizing the illusion of total knowledge, one creates a sense of mastery—particularly when that comprehensiveness is based on a new combination of different fields of knowledge. Think of the combination of classical and medieval knowledge that helped generate the Renaissance, with its ambitious totalizing projects, such as Sir Walter Raleigh's five-volume *History of the World* (1614), which did not even get past 130 BCE, or Roger Bacons's encyclopedic *Major Opus (Operis Majoris, 1268)*, which was to include everything known. Or consider the combination of sensory knowledge and formal abstraction in Friedrich Schiller's concept of the "play drive," which yields a unique sense of wholeness and mastery that may explain some of the pleasures of contemporary game culture and why so many multimedia works cultivate the illusion of wholeness:

> It is precisely play and play alone, which of all man's states and conditions is the one which makes him whole and unfolds both sides of his nature at once. . . . Man only plays when he is in the fullest sense of the word a human being, and he is only fully a human being when he plays (15th Letter, 425).

When database narrative is combined with digital culture, it potentially promises a similar utopian mastery. For example, when Labyrinth was designing *The Danube Exodus: The Rippling Currents of the River*, an earlier installation on

Jewish history produced in collaboration with Hungarian artist Peter Forgács, we went from his sixty-minute video documentary, aired on European television, to an immersive installation based on some forty hours of footage. Yet, we still considered the value of this expanded footage to be more dependent on its rarity than its abundance, and therefore chose to emphasize the gaps. As a consequence, museum visitors had to take a more active role in generating narratives that could accommodate the images, sounds and words they encountered in the exhibition's expanding narrative field.

This emphasis on the gaps is also well suited to *Jewish Homegrown History*. That is why we begin with Jews in California, where the cultural history is especially full of holes. This project collects new data from ordinary people (having them tell their stories) and creates a dialogue between these personal memories and what is already known (through published history). Never relying on any single authority or any authoritative "voice-of-god" documentary, our history repeatedly confronts users with conflicting data from multiple sources. As in our previous Labyrinth projects, the primary challenge for the individual user is to find a new narrative premise that can accommodate the data that our project collects and remixes, or at least as much of it as the user has seen and heard.

THE ON-LINE DIALOGUE BETWEEN PERSONAL MEMORIES AND PUBLISHED HISTORY

Unlike other on-line participatory sites where users can record their family histories, our multimedia archive focuses on generating a productive dialogue between the personal memories being contributed (stories, family photos, home movies) and the broader published history (based on scholarly books, essays, newspaper articles, interviews, archival photographs, newsreels, documents) that contextualize these personal contributions. Thus, it creates a unique mode of interactive history that enables contributors to see the immediate effect of their own digital storytelling on the public record and the process by which it enriches, complicates or challenges what is known. The experience provides two kinds of pleasure—an immediate narcissistic engagement with one's own genealogy and experience but also a broader interest and engagement in understanding the implicit, larger historical patterns. By encouraging families to collaborate on telling their stories and to "publish" them through this user-friendly interface, this narrative mode of data collection fosters a meaningful form of trans-generational learning.

This unique dialogue also generates for each user a personalized database narrative on the fly—not only by gathering historical modules from the public record that are relevant to an individual's own family stories but also by empowering the user to choose which modules to watch or preserve. It makes historiography accessible to the general public, enabling them to become active participants in the dynamic interplay between past and present, and between personal memories and collective history.

This unique dialogic process is made possible by our "homegrown history" application, which we are making available to others as free open-source software. Thus, our project has two goals: to present a visually compelling and historically rigorous cultural history of Jews in America, and to provide an innovative national model that can be applied to other subjects. Although this "homegrown history" software was originally designed to show the distinctive nature of the Jewish experience, we have developed it so that it can easily be adapted to other ethnic groups. We believe this duality helps to demonstrate how Jews are deeply connected to the rest of the world.

When we began this project, we saw this dialogue as analogous to the struggle described by post-colonialist theorist Homi Bhaba—between an official "pedagogic" history imposed on a nation to create unity and order versus a "performative" history emerging from disempowered people on the margins to reaffirm their own complexity and difference.[3] But instead of emphasizing this binary relationship between top-down and bottom-up forms of history, we realized (after discussions with many historians on our Advisory Board) that it was more productive to challenge the fixed boundaries between personal and "official" history. We used three strategies to blur these boundaries: featuring excerpts from scholarly histories and documentaries that use personal testimonies as primary evidence,[4] allowing contributions of other users to function as published history, and asking scholarly interviewees to describe their own family histories. We remain committed to an open-ended performative history that leverages the gaps in our knowledge as a driving force of inquiry.

What does this mean in concrete terms for users of the on-line archive? If users choose the **Collecting Mode**, they fill out a brief questionnaire that enables them to contribute information about themselves and their families.[5] The first set of questions asks them to trace their family immigration trajectories from the earliest known point of origin, to the location where they are now living. An open text-box enables them to explain the reasons why each person left each particular site, and why they chose the next location. Depending on their knowledge of family history, they can fill out this information for as many individuals as they want and for as many locations as they need. Alternatively, they can return to and revise their stories after they have gathered more information. After inputting this information, their family trajectories appear on the map as color-coded lines connecting the various cities where they have lived (see Figure 1). This interactive map enables users to see how their own storytelling becomes part of the public record. They also see how their trajectories intersect with those entered by other users.

Figure 1: *The family trajectories of contributors appear on the map as color-coded lines connecting the various cities where they have lived. This interactive map enables users to see the impact of their own storytelling on the public record.*

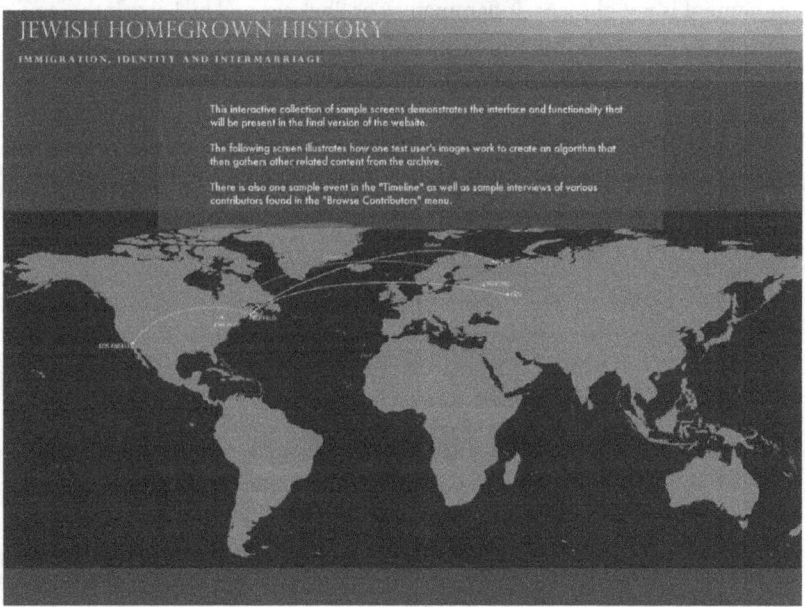

The second set of questions concern the current location of oneself and one's family. After naming the city and state where they now reside and the year when they first settled there, they are asked to describe their first neighborhood in this city and how it has changed. The third set of questions concern identity. Where did you go to school? What kind of work do you do? How would you describe you or your family's relationship to Judaism? Are you currently a member of a synagogue? Do you speak Yiddish or Hebrew? Is there intermarriage in your family? What is your own attitude towards intermarriage between Jews and non-Jews? You are then asked: what story best captures you or your family's experience as Jews living in your city.

Most of these questions are open-ended, which means users decide how brief or how long to make their stories. They also decide whether they want to upload a series of photographs or excerpts from home movies (see Figure 2). They are asked to include a caption for each photograph and to provide some basic metadata (year, location, names of people, themes, events), which will function as searchable key words for these contributions. Before any of this data can become part of the "public record" on the website, the contributor must check a box granting Labyrinth non-exclusive world rights to exhibit these materials on-line and in its installations and to make them part of USC's Digital Archive. The data will also be reviewed by monitors to make sure that the content is not obscene, inflammatory or libelous, and by Labyrinth's staff to select those materials that will be included in the museum installation.

Figure 2: *Contributors decide whether they want to upload a series of photographs and whether they want to contribute excerpts from home movies. They are asked to include a caption for each photograph and to provide some basic metadata (year, location, names of people, themes, events), which will function as searchable key words for these contributions.*

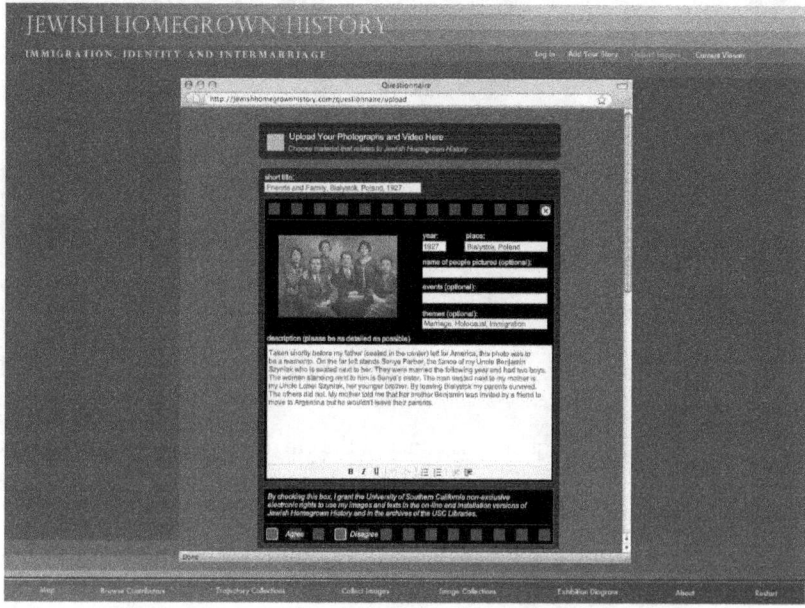

Once a contributor completes the password-protected questionnaire and uploads family photographs and home movies, our "homegrown history" software follows a programmed protocol to collect materials from the archive that are related to these contributions. Using pre-selected key words (e.g., events, themes, places, proper names), the program uses an algorithm to make these automated selections (see Figure 3). The user is then able to select and view any of these materials in the **Content Viewer**, or save any of them for later retrieval. Providing an historical scaffolding of archival information about a particular period and place, these collected materials contextualize the user's own personal experience; and, conversely, the user's personal contributions give Labyrinth an opportunity to enrich, complicate or qualify what is already in the existing database.

Figure 3: *This diagram shows how the dialogue between personal contributions and historical modules works. Once a contributor completes the questionnaire and uploads images, our "homegrown history" software follows a programmed protocol to collect materials from the database that are related to these materials. Using pre-selected key words (e.g., events, themes, places, proper names), the program uses an algorithm to make these automated selections.*

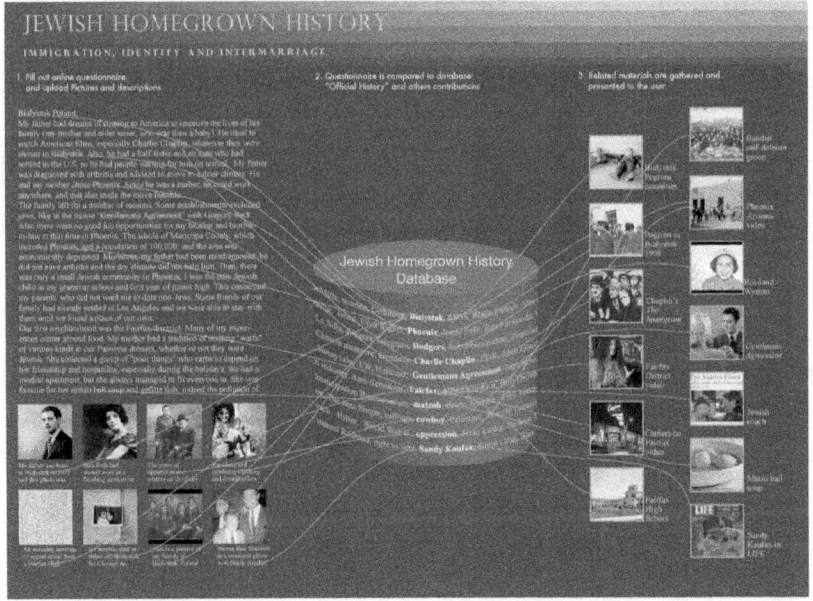

We see this encounter as "dialogic" in the Bahktinian sense: examples from both kinds of history (the personal and the published) become enriched through juxtaposition, and their meanings are redefined in the process. As M. Bahktin puts it: "The linguistic significance of a given utterance is understood against the background of language, while its actual meaning is understood against the background of other concrete utterances on the same theme, a background made up of contradictory opinions, points of view and value judgments" (281).

THE CASE OF ROSALIE NEWELL

To consider how this dialogic process works for individual users, we will examine a few specific stories, photographs, and home movies contributed by one user and see what materials they call up from the archive and how meanings are changed in the process. As our case study we will use Rosalie Newell, a 71-year-old Jewish woman currently living in the Fairfax district of Los Angeles (see Figure 4).

Rosalie's descriptions of her family's experience in Bialystok call up vivid passages from *The Bialystoker Memorial Book*, with accompanying images and detailed accounts of the deadly pogroms that made her parents want to flee Poland. This source also describes the historic role played by the Bund (the Jewish Union) in Bialystok, including their efforts to save fellow Jews from these anti-Jewish race riots. The Bund is described as secular and anti-Zionist, yet committed to Yiddish culture, which might help contextualize Rosalie's own combination of secularism (what she calls "missing the faith gene") and her immersion in *Yiddishkeit*, a combination she previously found difficult to explain.

Figure 4: *Rosalie Newell's stories and family photographs call up historical modules from many different sources, each represented by a thumbnail image. She can choose which ones to open and which ones to preserve.*

Although her family first settled in Chicago where Rosalie was born, most of her vivid childhood memories come from Arizona, where they moved because her father was asthmatic. Rosalie's stories about her family's experience in Phoenix during the 1940s begin with the rush of pleasure she felt when first experiencing the wide-open spaces of Arizona (particularly in contrast with the urban density of Chicago). These stories are accompanied by a photograph of her and her niece dressed in cowgirl outfits. This image calls up a passage from Sean Griffin's essay "Kings of the Wild Backyard: Davy Crockett and Children's Space," which explains how suburban parents during the postwar period tried to give their children a sense of liberty while still carefully restricting their spatial mobility to the backyard. The image also retrieves a similar period photograph from another contributor, showing her participation in the same Western costuming fad. Griffin's text might encourage Rosalie to search these two photographs (and her memories) for signs that would support (or contradict) his claim that "girls used the 'cowgirl' in order to complicate the gender boundaries that were already impinging on them.... [for] at least some girls were ignoring how the adult world would have preferred them to use Davy's image" (Griffin 115–17).

Rosalie's claim that her family decided to leave Phoenix partly because she had no Jewish friends and they feared she might end up marrying a gentile, calls up an excerpt from Isaac Artenstein's documentary, *Frontier Jews*, on the history of Jews in Tucson, Tombstone and other parts of Arizona. The oral histories in this excerpt might make her question whether her family's fears were well-grounded. Yet her story makes us notice that Artenstein's film does not cover Phoenix. In other words, both her family story and Artenstein's clip call attention to gaps in their respective contributions which we might otherwise fail to notice.

When Rosalie claims her father wanted to move to Los Angeles partly in hope of meeting Charlie Chaplin, she then adds "probably he was just joking." These comments call up three items that suggest he may not have been kidding after all: a textual passage from J. Hoberman's essay, "The First 'Jewish' Superstar: Charlie Chaplin" which explains why Chaplin (a non-Jew) appealed to so many Jewish immigrants; a brief segment from an on-screen interview with USC historian Steven J. Ross claiming that Chaplin was frequently identified as a Jewish immigrant; and an excerpt from *Three Winters in the Sun: Einstein in California,* an earlier Labyrinth project, indicating that the person whom Jewish scientist Albert Einstein most wanted to meet in California was also Charlie Chaplin, with whom he closely identified.[6]

Rosalie's description of her teenage years in the Fairfax district, a Jewish enclave of Los Angeles, calls up related passages about the neighborhood from Stephen Sass' book, *Jewish Los Angeles—A Guide* (1982), Lynn Kronzek's "Fairfax: A Home, a Community, and a Way of Life" (1990), and Deborah Dash Moore's *To the Golden Cities: Pursuing the American Jewish Dream in Miami and L.A.* (1996), each with accompanying archival stills from USC Libraries' Special Collections. It also retrieves recent interviews with Nira Levy Maslin, a Yemenite Jewish émigré from Israel who runs a tea-shop on Fairfax Avenue that features African drumming and is part of the "Jewish Renaissance"; and with independent scholar Lynn Kronzek, who describes the early suburban days of the Fairfax area before it became a Jewish enclave and tells how living in that district in the 1980s helped make her husband decide to become a rabbi.

In addition to her stories and photographs, Rosalie contributed two home movies she made herself in 1995, both featuring her mother at age ninety, still living in the Fairfax area. One shows her mother making a potato kugel, which calls up a passage by cultural historian Barbara Kirshenblatt-Gimblett (whose family also came from Poland), describing typical Jewish food preparations from Eastern Europe. This excerpt comes from a book she wrote with her father, the painter Mayer Kirshenblatt, which makes us attend to the collaborative dimension in Rosalie's movie as well. While highlighting her mother's talents as a cook, Rosalie was also developing her own new talent as a videographer. Rosalie's second movie shows her mother reading an article in Yiddish from the *Forward*, a Jewish-American newspaper published in separate Yiddish and English editions. Describing the influx of Russian émigré Jews moving into the Fairfax district during the late 1980s and 1990s, this article evokes a clip from Lynne Littman's film *In Her Own Time* (1985), which documents Barbara Myerhoff's ethnographic study of the Russian orthodox Jewish community living in the same Fairfax area. While Rosalie's 90-year old mother sympathized with these orthodox Jews, yet felt distant from them culturally, Myerhoff was drawn to their spirituality and strong sense of community, particularly as she herself was in a final battle against lung cancer. Still, both collaborations show the filmmaker (whether a professional like Littman or an amateur like Rosalie) expressing her love for her vibrant subject by documenting her courageous engagement with the outside world—even while nearing death.

Within her stories about living in the Fairfax district, Rosalie gives a detailed account of her own experience at Fairfax High School in the 1950s when the student body was predominantly Jewish and when she had teachers who were intellectually demanding. This description brings forth a brief film (made by Labyrinth), citing a passage from Moore's *To the Golden Cities* that confirms Fairfax was one of the few places in Southern California where one could find a Jewish public school and that it was also one of the first to offer Hebrew as a foreign language. Yet this film also points out that neither the Wikipedia entry on Fairfax High, nor the school's own official website mentions its past associations with the Jewish community. Instead, these contemporary websites describe Fairfax as an inner city school that experienced "white flight" during the 1980s and that now has a predominantly Latino and African American student body. In making this participatory history, we feel it is essential to include excerpts not only from scholarly sources but also from popular participatory sites such as Wikipedia. But, as in this example of Fairfax High School, we also feel compelled to show what is sometimes omitted from those sites. As if to reconcile the differences among these various accounts, the program also calls up an interview with a young "Jewish Latina," who attended Fairfax in the 1980s, and claims it was very diverse from an ethnic standpoint, and, in particular, included Jews from all over the world. It also retrieves a front-page article from the *Los Angeles Times* (Getlin) about Rosalie's favorite history teacher Marty Biegel, an Orthodox Jew who later became the basketball coach. In 1969 Biegel played an historical role in easing the city's racial tensions, when he helped integrate Fairfax High by encouraging the new black students (then being bussed across the city) to play on the basketball team. This started a new era of athletic achievement for Fairfax, which had formerly been known only for its champion chess team.

One of Rosalie's most "treasured" contributions is her family photograph of her nephew with Jewish pitcher Sandy Koufax, who played for the Los Angeles Dodgers. Besides being ardent baseball fans, her family admired Koufax for refusing to pitch at the opening game of the World Series, when it fell on Yom Kippur. This photograph brings forward two historical modules from the archive that present a less favorable perspective toward the Dodgers' move to Los Angeles and toward some of the Jews who made it happen. One is an archival photograph showing Los Angeles Councilwoman Rosalind Weiner Wyman from the Fairfax District (the youngest person and first Jew to sit on the Council), with the city fathers, signing the agreement that promised to build the new Dodger Stadium that would bring them from Brooklyn. This photograph is accompanied by a passage from Moore's *To The Golden Cities* that describes the bitter conflict that developed between Weiner (who received death threats) and her former liberal Latino ally, Edward Roybal of Boyle Heights, over the destruction of public housing in Chavez Ravine, which was done in order to make way for the stadium. The program also brings up an archival photograph of Rose Chernin (Executive Director of the Los Angeles Committee for the Protection of the Foreign Born [LACPFB]) with an excerpt from historian George Sanchez's award-winning essay "What's Good for Boyle Heights Is Good for the Jews," which provides an even harsher account of Weiner's break from her former liberal stance and her alleged alliance with leftist causes in Boyle Heights.

> Often discussed as the second liberal on the council in the 1950s—joining Edward Roybal from Boyle Heights—Wyman critically shaped her political ideology from the postwar suburban sensibilities of Los Angeles's Westside liberalism. While this liberalism included moderate support for civil rights efforts in the city, it also was staunchly anticommunist. Wyman joined the vast majority of her colleagues after 1952 in viewing public housing, for example, as a suspicious socialist experiment, and she led efforts within the city council from 1956 to 1958 in handing over Chavez Ravine to Walter O'Malley to facilitate the move of the Brooklyn Dodgers to Los Angeles (653).

Sanchez shows that Wyman's conflicts with the more radical Jewish community in Boyle Heights were not limited to the struggle over Chavez Ravine. He reports how in 1958 she presented a citation to two FBI undercover agents, Marion and Paul Miller, who gave evidence about the "inner workings of the Los Angeles Committee for the Protection of the Foreign Born" during the early 1950s. This citation incensed the LACPFB and "especially its executive director, Rose Chernin, who . . . orchestrated a letter-writing campaign to the city council, particularly directed at Wyman." This incident also brings forth a related interview with Esther Raucher, who grew up in the leftist Jewish community of City Terrace (near Boyle Heights) but who attended Fairfax High in the late 1950s, where she became friends with Rosalie Newell. In the interview Raucher describes a class reunion in City Terrace where she confronted the son of FBI agents (like the Millers), who had been responsible for sending the parents of some of their schoolmates to prison. Interestingly, although Rosalie Newell and Esther Raucher were allied to different sides of this conflict, they had never discussed these episodes from Los Angeles Jewish history until this program brought the relevant modules together.

What emerges from this particular collection of historical modules is a database narrative about the Fairfax district as a Los Angeles neighborhood that became an important Jewish enclave around the end of World War II. Fairfax remained so in later decades, as it continued to attract more Orthodox

Jews (particularly from Russia during the 1980s and 1990s), many of whom sent their children to Jewish schools rather than to public schools like Fairfax High. Yet ever since the late 1960s, this Fairfax district also continued to display a growing range of ethnic diversity, especially encompassing Latinos and African Americans, whose relations with Jews became more complex. While Rosalie Newell might choose to watch and read only some of these contextualizing materials, they would all be available as possible modules for her own personalized database narrative.

BROWSING THE TIMELINE

Instead of contributing their family stories like Rosalie Newell, some users who come to the on-line archive may choose the **Browsing Mode,** which enables them to explore the historical materials we have already collected. A **Search Engine** enables them to request specific names, places, and themes, a request that brings forth all relevant archival materials (texts, images, interviews, charts, film clips, sound files—both from the published history and personal stories) related to a given key word or words. From these targeted materials, the user then selects the ones she wants to see and in what order, selections that can be played within the **Content Viewer.** The browsing user can also choose historical events from the timeline, whether they are global, national or local in context. Given that the archive will be accessible worldwide, a drop-down menu will enable users to select which location will be designated the local site, to which all other data will be related.

For example, if a user selects the "1906 San Francisco Earthquake and Fire" from the timeline as a local California event (see Figure 5), the program will gather the following modules: Ava Kahn's 1988 interview with the late Reva Aronson, who was six at the time of the earthquake and whose family sought refuge in Golden Gate Park; a brief movie that features a passage from Harriet Lane Levy's memoir, *920 O'Farrell Street: A Jewish Girlhood in Old San Francisco* read in voice-over, describing what she saw when she returned home to San Francisco after the fire, with archival images showing the devastation and what buildings later replaced her home; an excerpt from our interview with Frances Dinkelspiel (author of *Towers of Gold: How One Jewish Immigrant Named Isaias Hellman Created California,* a meticulously researched biography of her great, great-grandfather; see her article elsewhere in this volume) explaining the impact of this disaster on Hellman and his family and on the banking industry, a number of brief period films of the devastation and its aftermath from the Library of Congress collection; a montage of stills of the damage from the USC archive, which are combined with first person accounts (including one by movie mogul Sol Lesser) collected by Rabbi William Kramer and by Ava Kahn; passages from Fred Rosenbaum's book *Visions of Reform: Congregation Emanu-El and the Jews of San Francisco, 1849-1999*, with accompanying still images, concerning the impact the earthquake had on the construction of synagogues in San Francisco; and an excerpt from an interview with California historian Kevin Starr, on how the devastation gave Jews in San Francisco a second chance to participate in building the city.

Figure 5: *If a user selects the "1906 San Francisco Earthquake and Fire" from the timeline, the program will gather from the database an array of historical materials, including archival images, interviews, historic films from the Library of Congress, first person accounts of those who survived it, and excerpts from published histories.*

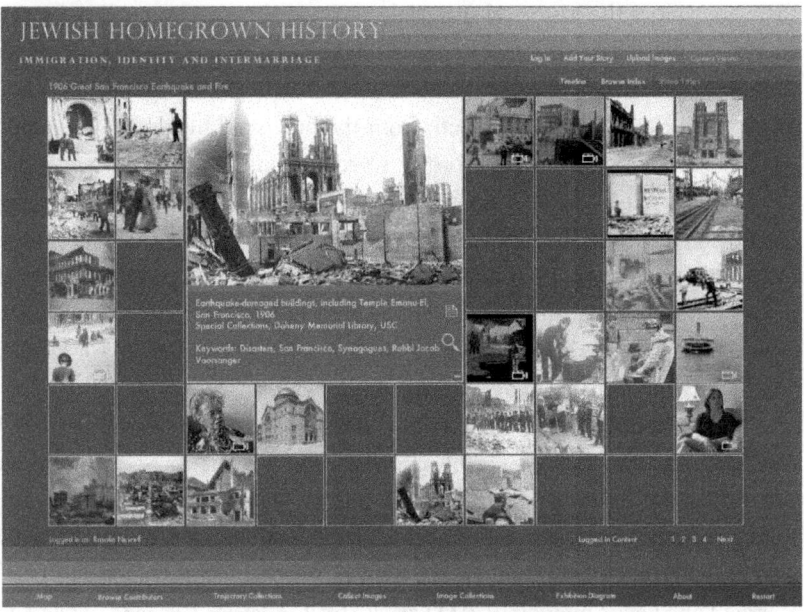

Although we have had to "seed" the archive during the early period of its development in order to collect the assets for the events listed in the timeline and to create the interactive dialogue between Rosalie's personal stories and the related published history modules they call up from the database, as the project grows, the making of connections of this nature will become easier because many of the associated materials will be coming from contributions by other users and by scholars who contribute excerpts from their own works. Yet, before the on-line archive is publicly launched, we will have modules of "official history" for all of the themes and for all of the events listed in the timeline.

JEWS IN THE GOLDEN STATE: THE CALIFORNIA PILOT

While this dialogic dimension between personal and public history is the unique feature of the on-line archive, it is our particular focus on the California perspective that distinguishes the traveling museum installation from other cultural histories of the Jews. By starting with the history of Jews in California (as opposed to Jews in New York, Chicago or Philadelphia, about which a good deal more is known and which is therefore far more familiar to the public), we leverage this gap in our knowledge as a rationale for developing a new line of inquiry.

This assumption that little is known about Jews in California is a conviction shared not only by the California historians on our Advisory Board such as Bill Deverell, Frances Dinkelspiel, Marc Dollinger, Ava Kahn, David Kaufman, Fred Rosenbaum, Kevin Starr, and Karen Wilson, but also by Jewish studies scholars based in the East—such as Hasia M. Diner, Barbara Kirschenblatt-Gimblett, Deborah Dash Moore, Jonathan Sarna, and Jeffrey Shandler. For example, when we interviewed California historian Kevin Starr, he argued that the "instant urbanism" experienced by San Francisco and Los Angeles was not characteristic of the growth patterns of large eastern cities like New York and Philadelphia, and that this acceleration was partly driven by the urbanism of German Jewish immigrants who came to California very early. When we interviewed "bicoastal" Jewish Studies scholar Moses Rischin, who had lived both in New York and California and later migrated from Los Angeles to San Francisco, he claimed that the concept of Jewish community was quite different in each of these locales—differences we plan to explore in detail. As we examined the complex interactions between Jews and Latinos in Los Angeles neighborhoods like Boyle Heights and the Fairfax District and in the border zones between San Diego and Tijuana, we realized these stories have not yet been told in depth and they are quite different from the interactions between Jews and Puerto Ricans, for example, in New York. We are contextualizing these gathered stories not only with work from Jewish studies scholars who are focusing on the west (like Ava Kahn and Marc Dollinger) but also from historians of the West (such as Bill Deverell, George Sanchez and Kevin Starr) whose previous works have not focused primarily on Jews. We are also searching the Shoah Institute Archives, now housed at USC, seeking testimonies of Holocaust survivors who settled in California after World War

II, finding out why they chose to come here, what kinds of Jewish communities they found, what kinds of experiences they had, and how they both enrich and complicate the story of Jews in the Golden State. We will follow the same strategy for selecting testimonies from those survivors who settled in New York, Philadelphia, Chicago and other cities, once the installation moves to the east.

By starting with a less traditional site for Jewish history like California, we also draw greater attention to the interplay among the local, the national, and the global aspects of the story. After the California pilot, each new exhibition will feature the locale in which it is exhibited (devoting around twenty-five to thirty percent of its materials to that specific location), while still retaining the national scope of the Jewish experience in the U.S. (which will then include the materials on California) and networked connections to international sites where Jews have lived throughout the world. The project demonstrates that all three contexts—the local, the national, and the global—are shifters whose meanings change, depending on the perspective of the viewer.

The installation will differ from the on-line archive by featuring a large-scale, multi-screen, curated presentation. In many ways, it will be modeled on *The Danube Exodus*, which premiered at the Getty Center in 2002 and has been traveling worldwide ever since. We believe the success of that earlier installation was based primarily on the immersive power of its images and sounds and the richness of the historical narrative they convey. These are also the qualities we are seeking in the installation version of *Jewish Homegrown History*, whose interactive dimensions will not be as central as they are on the on-line archive but whose sensory presentation will be far more compelling.

When visitors first enter the exhibition space, they will pass by a kiosk that invites them to use a very simple interface to enter basic information about the immigration trajectories of their own families. Once submitted, this information will be instantly displayed as animated lines that are visible on a world map, projected onto the floor. The display of this personal information will not only establish the groundwork for what is to come but also make the visitor feel more personally involved in the exhibition. Ten visitor trajectories will be visible on the floor with only the latest being highlighted at any given time. All of the trajectories will be collected over the run of the exhibition, and an updated summary of this data will be displayed at all times within the exhibition space.

The installation will also feature a series of documentary film screenings on related subjects, along with the best of the home movies we collect. These screenings will take place in a separate room (with seating) near the primary exhibition space.

Once visitors move deeper into the main exhibition area, they will see three large (six foot by eight foot) screens, each fronted by an accompanying touch-screen monitor. The individual monitors will display at least ten icons per screen. If no one has made a selection from one of the touch-screens, each main screen will display a brief (five to seven minute) film loop on one of the project's three main sub-themes. The screen on the left will display a film loop about "Immigration & Migration," the center screen about "Identity & Cultural Contributions," and the screen on the right about "Intermarriage & Other Alliances." These three film loops will have little or no dialogue (though they might have an occasional brief text or inter-title), and will all work with one ambient sound track that will be heard throughout the space.

As soon as a visitor selects an icon displayed on a touch-screen monitor, a mini-narrative (what we call a thematic "orchestration") will interrupt all three film loops (starting with the large screen that the interactor is directly facing and then spreading to the others) as it plays out across all three large screens. Since this selection will control both the images and sounds and determine what everyone in the room is experiencing, the user will suddenly be positioned as a performer. The selection process will work like a jukebox, with the chosen orchestrations (each no more than three to five minutes in length) queuing up in sequential order for playback. Although it will not be possible to interrupt an orchestration while it is playing, other selections can be explored and chosen on the other two touch-screen monitors. This dynamic ensures that visitors take turns and that no single person gets two choices in a row. Given that each monitor will have a different set of icons that trigger different orchestrations, users will be encouraged to move from one monitor to another.

Each thematic orchestration will combine archival images and footage, excerpts from documentaries and original interviews, brief textual quotations and voice-over commentaries, music and ambient sounds, and the best of what we have gleaned from family photographs, home movies and stories collected on the website and during "home-movie" collection days we are hosting throughout the state. New modules will be added during the four-month run of the exhibition, so that more recent contributions to the website can be incorporated into the installation. This "updating" process will also enable us to adapt the installation more easily to new exhibition sites—not only in California (in Berkeley and San Diego) but also in Philadelphia, New York and other venues across the nation, thereby enriching the interplay among the local, national and global contexts for the various themes.

Given that each touch-screen monitor displays approximately ten icons, each of which triggers a brief thematic orchestration (three to five minutes in length), there will be a minimum of ninety minutes of video. Whenever a visitor rolls over an icon, a brief text will appear that explains what that particular orchestration will cover, thereby helping the user make a selection.

Although each large screen and its accompanying touch-screen monitor will be linked to one of the sub-themes, all of the thematic orchestrations are designed to demonstrate the rich interplay among these issues of Immigration, Identity and Intermarriage. Similarly, although the issues of *Immigration & Migration* stress global connections, while *Identity & Cultural Contributions* emphasize the Jewish legacy for the nation, and *Intermarriage & Other Alliances* explore attitudes and close relations with other ethnic groups within a specific locale, the installation is constructed to show that all of these positions are shifters whose meanings depend on the user's perspective and point of view. In this way, visitors experience the installation as a database narrative, whose meanings keep changing depending on how the thematic orchestrations are remixed.

Some orchestrations in the installation will leverage discoveries that open new lines of inquiry. For example, one theme that emerged during our research is the important role that Jewish Americans have played in the information, computer and communications technology industries, particularly within California—a story that has never been fully told. We started to address this issue in our interview with Jack Tramiel (now in his 90s), the founder of Commodore Computers, who later bought Atari and who witnessed the dramatic rise of Silicon Valley. We are now following this up by doing interviews with several other figures in this field, including USC Viterbi Professor of Engineering Solomon Wolf Golomb, who, while supervising a telecommunications research group at the Jet Propulsion Laboratory in the late 1950s, played a major role in designing deep-space communications for lunar and planetary explorations. Perhaps best known to the general public for his invention of polyominoes, that inspired the popular computer game *Tetris*, he has received many awards for his exceptional contributions to information sciences and systems over the past four decades, and more specifically, for applying advanced mathematics to problems in digital communications. Golomb claims that his early Talmudic training helped him master mathematics and information theory, not because it followed the same logic but because it was another kind of logical system that was equally demanding. We are exploring how extensive the role of Jewish Americans has been in this field; what, if any, has been the role played by Israeli émigrés; and what aspects of Jewish culture have contributed to this pattern.

As in the on-line archive, knowledge production in the installation will depend primarily on a montage of images. But, how does one develop an argument primarily through images while still retaining the plurality of meanings that every photograph and filmic image carries? As Roland Barthes has argued in his essay "The Rhetoric of the Image":

> In every society various techniques are developed intended to *fix* the floating chain of signifieds in such a way as to counter the terror of uncertain signs; the linguistic message is one of these techniques ... The caption ... helps me to choose *the correct level of perception*, permits me to focus not simply my gaze but also my understanding. ... The text has thus a *repressive* value and we can see that it is at this level that the morality and ideology of a society are above all invested (38–40).

While we want to direct the readings of these images, we do not want to suppress their pluralistic meanings through the imposition of too many voice-overs and inter-titles. Instead we want to broaden the range of meanings through interplay between text and image, sound and visualization. This interplay also demands a reliance on dialectic montage—where the whole is greater than the sum of the parts. This concept was theorized not only by the great filmmaker Sergei Eisenstein (whose subject was always history), but also by Bakhtin, whose ideas on the dialogic potential of multi-voiced forms laid the groundwork for intertextuality and also for database narrative.

For example, as we take the cluster of historical modules that are retrieved from the database for the 1906 San Francisco Earthquake and Fire in the on-line archive, and transform them into a brief (three to five minute) orchestration (or mini-narrative) for the three large screens in the installation, our editing of these materials will develop a particular reading of that event. The combination of image, voice and sound might emphasize that this natural disaster gave Jews an opportunity to participate more fully in rebuilding the city and in designing a more dramatic presence for the Jewish community—a perspective that would be particularly apparent in tracing the impact of what happened to the synagogues (as described by Fred Rosenbaum). On the other hand, it might also be possible to see these disastrous events as unifying all San Franciscans, because they all had experienced the same trauma. According to Frances Dinkelspiel, even a rich Jewish banker—like Isaias W. Hellman and his family—stood in the soup lines and sought refuge in Golden Gate Park. And once they had endured and survived this disaster, what kinds of new safety measures and new public pleasures were designed for the rugged citizens of this city? In what ways did this disaster and its aftermath contribute to the increasing assimilation of Jews in San Francisco? Our orchestration will interweave both readings, as they play across the three large screens.

Montage will also be central to an orchestration on generational conflicts between parents and children, particularly over issues of orthodoxy and religious practice. As a starting point we discovered striking parallel sequences from two of the documentaries that will be included in our series—Lynne Littman's *In Her Own Time* (1985), which documents Barbara Myerhoff's ethnographic study of orthodox Jews living in LA's Fairfax district, and Lisa M. Kors's *Shayna Maidels* (1991), which tells the story of teenage Jewish orthodox girls attending YULA (the Yeshiva University of Los Angeles) and the religious conflicts they have with their parents who are less orthodox than they are. Both films feature a powerful sequence in which a mother and daughter confront each other, yet the religious alignments are reversed: in Littman's film it is the mother who is orthodox, whereas in Kors' film it is the daughter. Yet both evoke an equally intense resentment in the other. While working on how we would use these parallel sequences in the orchestration and draw on their similar visual compositions, we discovered by sheer coincidence that the mother in *Shayna Maidels* was the ex-wife of historian George Sanchez, whom we had interviewed a few days after first watching the film but without knowing the connection. Following our strategy of asking all scholars we interview to tell us about their own family history, I asked Sanchez to describe his own relationship to Judaism. He told us that he had converted from Catholicism to Judaism while he was married to his ex-wife who was Jewish, and he also spoke with pride about having two Jewish step-daughters, one of whom (the orthodox teen featured in Kors's film) was now living in Israel.

This coincidence involving Sanchez strengthened the connection of these two films (neither of which mentions intermarriage) with a more recent documentary that does, Lisa Leeman's *Out of Faith* (2008), which focuses on generational conflict within a Jewish family in Chicago. While the first generation (the grandmother and grandfather) were Holocaust survivors, the second generation was born in Israel, and two from the third generation married outside the faith. Although the grandmother accepts her granddaughter's marriage to a Christian, she disowns her grandson for doing the same thing. Still, the film presents the grandmother in a sympathetic light. We can understand her reasons for condemning intermarriage, particularly in light of her own experiences in the death camp and the promises she made to those who did not survive. Though the grandson refused to be interviewed on camera, we hear his speech at his grandmother's funeral. While watching these moving scenes with the grandmother from *Out of Faith*, I could not help thinking of an anecdote (recounted with some irony and humor) in our interview with USC Historian Steve Ross, whose mother (also a survivor of Auschwitz) told him, when he asked her, at the age of thirty, whether she would mind if he married a non-Jew: "No, I won't mind, I'll just stick my head in the oven and turn on the gas."

By reading *Out of Faith* in juxtaposition with the other two films (*Shayna Maidels* and *In Her Own Time*), I realized that the basic transgenerational dynamics were far more important than they might otherwise have appeared. Instead of following the anticipated generational alternation between orthodoxy and secularism (as occurs in *Shayna Maidels* and *In her Own Time*), the family in *Out of Faith* continues to move farther away from orthodoxy. Perhaps that helps explain why the grandmother was so much harsher on her grandson than she was on her granddaughter, because *his* father had also married a Christian, but one (unlike her daughter-in-law) who had converted to Judaism. Thus, although the grandmother had suppressed her anger toward her son in light of that conversion, it was now unleashed with double intensity on her grandson. These transgenerational dynamics are perhaps best understood when one looks at all of these texts together, and in light of the passage from Jonathan Sarna already quoted at the beginning of this essay (see p. 97).

ON WORDS AND IMAGES

From these descriptions of how the interactive on-line archive and the immersive installation will function, it becomes clear that we are not really *writing* a cultural history about Jews in California, or Jews in America. Rather we have designed a transmedia structure—an information system—that gathers and combines the contributions of scholars, archivists, documentary filmmakers and the general public in productive ways and that engages this social network in an on-going process that will continue generating new historical narratives about Jews in America long after the California pilot closes. This is another sense in which our project becomes *Jewish Homegrown History*.

Notes

*. For a link to larger versions of this and other illustrations see http://casdeninstitute.usc.edu/resources/publications/the_jewish_role_in_american_li_6/.
1. For a brief history of the Labyrinth Project, see Jeffrey Shaw and Peter Weibel, eds., *Future Cinema: The Cinematic Imaginary after Film*, 342–59. Also visit Labyrinth's website: <www.thelabyrinthproject.com>.
2. For example, in *The Language of New Media*, Lev Manovich writes: "I prefer to think of them as two competing imaginations, two basic creative impulses, two essential responses to the world.... Modern media is the new battlefield for the competition between database and narrative" (233–34).
3. Bhabha also acknowledges the productive interplay between these two kinds of history: "In the production of the nation as narration there is a split between the continuist, accumulative temporality of the pedagogical, and the repetitious, recursive strategy of the performative. It is through this process of splitting that the conceptual ambivalence of modern society becomes the site of *writing the nation*" (297).
4. Two examples are *Jewish Voices of the California Gold Rush: A Documentary History, 1849–1880*, a wide range of first-hand accounts collected and edited by historian Ava F. Kahn; and Harriet Lane Levy's *920 O'Farrell Street: A Jewish Girlhood in Old San Francisco*, a lively memoir of an affluent young Jewish woman from San Francisco who was a good friend of Alice B. Toklas.
5. Although not a complete version with full functionality, a prototype of the questionnaire can be found at <http://jewishhomegrownhistory.com>.
6. To learn more about Labyrinth's *Three Winters in the Sun: Einstein in California*, see: <http://college.usc.edu/labyrinth/einstein/einstein.html>; Teicholz; and Kinder, Kang and Kratky.

Works Cited

Bakhtin, M. M. *The Dialogic Imagination: Four Essays by M. M. Bakhtin.* Ed. Michael Holquist. Trans. Caryl Emerson and Michael Holquist. Austin: Univ. of Texas, 1981.

Barthes, Roland. "Rhetoric of the Image." *Image, Music, Text: Essays Selected and Translated by Stephen Heath.* New York: Noonday, 1977. 32–51.

Bhabha, Homi K. "DissemiNation: Time, Narrative, and the Margins of the Modern Nation." *Nation and Narration.* Ed. Homi K. Bhabha. London and New York: Routledge, 1990. 291–322.

Deleuze, Gilles. *Cinema 2: The Time-Image.* Trans. Hugh Tomlinson and Robert Galeta. Minneapolis: Univ. of Minnesota, 2001.

Dinkelspiel, Frances. *Towers of Gold: How One Jewish Immigrant Named Isaias Hellman Created California.* New York: St. Martin's, 2008.

Diner, Hasia M. *The Jews of the United States, 1654 to 2000.* Berkeley and Los Angeles: Univ. of California, 2004.

"Fairfax High School." *Wikipedia.* Sept. 17, 2009 <http://en.wikipedia.org/wiki/Fairfax_High_School_(Los Angeles)>.

Fairfax High School. 2009. <www.fairfaxhs.org/>.

Forgács, Péter and The Labyrinth Project. *The Danube Exodus: The Rippling Currents of the River.* Sept. 30, 2009 <http://college.usc.edu/labyrinth/forgacs/forgacs.html/; *Artabase.* Sept. 30, 2009 <http://artabase.net/exhibition/1353-the-danube-exodus-the-rippling-currents>; The J. Paul Getty Museum, Los Angeles. Aug. 17–Sept. 29, 2002 <http://www.getty.edu/art/exhibitions/danube/>; The Judah L. Magnes Museum, Berkeley. Sept. 12, 2005–Jan. 22, 2006 <http://www.magnes.org/exhibits/danube.htm>; Jewish Museum Berlin. April 20–Aug. 26, 2007 <http://www.juedisches-museum-berlin.de/site/EN/01-Exhibitions/02-Special-Exhibitions/04-All-Special-Exhibitions/Exhibitions/danube-exodus/danube-exodus.php>; The Jewish Museum, New York. March 15–Aug. 2, 2009 <http://www.thejewishmuseum.org/exhibitions/danubeexodus>.

Frontier Jews. Dir. Isaac Artentstein, forthcoming.

Griffin, Sean. "Kings of the Wild Backyard: Davy Crockett and Children's Space." *Kids' Media Culture.* Ed. Marsha Kinder. Durham and London: Duke Univ., 1999. 102–21.

Hoberman, J. "The First 'Jewish' Superstar: Charlie Chaplin." *Entertaining America: Jews, Movies, and Broadcasting.* Ed. J. Hoberman and Jeffrey Shandler. Princeton: Princeton Univ., 2003. 34–39.

In Her Own Time. Dir. Lynne Littman. Direct Cinema Limited, 1985.

Jewish Homegrown History. 2009. *The Labyrinth Project*, University of Southern California's School of Cinematic Arts. Sept. 30, 2009 <http://www.jewishhomegrownhistory.com/>.

Kahn, Ava F. *Jewish Voices of the California Gold Rush: A Documentary History, 1849–1880.* Ed. Ava F. Kahn. Detroit: Wayne State Univ., 2002.

Kirshenblatt, Mayer and Kirshenblatt-Gimblett, Barbara. *They Called Me Mayer July: Painted Memories of a Jewish Childhood in Poland before the Holocaust.* Berkeley and Los Angeles: Univ. of California, 2007.

Kronzek, Lynn C. "Fairfax: A Home, a Community, a Way of Life." *Legacy, Journal of the Jewish Historical Society of Southern California* 1.4 (Spring 1990).

The Labyrinth Project. 2009. University of Southern California's School of Cinematic Arts. Sept. 30, 2009 <http://www.thelabyrinthproject.com>.

Kinder, Marsha, Kang, Kristy H. A., and Kratky, Andreas. *Three Winters in the Sun: Einstein in California.* Book and DVD-ROM. Los Angeles: USC-Annenberg Center for Communication, 2005.

The Labyrinth Project. *Three Winters in the Sun: Einstein in California.* University of Southern California. Sept. 30, 2009 <http://college.usc.edu/labyrinth/einstein/einstein.html>.

Getlin, Josh. "On Court and Off, He Made Them Winners." *Los Angeles Times* Dec. 12, 2008: A1.

Levy, Harriet Lane. *920 O'Farrell Street: A Jewish Girlhood in Old San Francisco.* New York: Doubleday, 1947.

Manovich, Lev. *The Language of New Media.* Cambridge and London: MIT, 2001.

Moore, Deborah Dash. *To the Golden Cities: Pursuing the American Jewish Dream in Miami and L.A.* Cambridge: Harvard Univ., 1996.

Night and Fog (Nuit et brouillard). Dir. Alain Resnais. Argos Films, 1955. English transcription Oct. 1, 2009 <http://www.uiowa.edu/~c08g001d/assignments/ngt-fog.html>.

Out of Faith. Dir. Lisa Leeman. PBS, 2008.

Rosenbaum, Fred. *Visions of Reform: Congregation Emanu-El and the Jews of San Francisco, 1849–1999.* Berkeley: Magnes Museum, 2000.

Sanchez, George, "What's Good for Boyle Heights is Good for the Jews: Creating Multiracialism on the Eastside during the 1950s." *American Quarterly* 56.3 (2004): 633–61.

Sarna, Jonathan D. *American Judaism: A History.* New Haven and London: Yale Univ., 2004.

Sass, Stephen J. *Jewish Los Angeles—a Guide: Everything Jewish under the Sun.* Los Angeles: Council on Jewish Life, 1982.

Schiller, Friedrich von. *On the Aesthetic Education of Man, in a Series of Letters.* Ed. and trans. E. M. Wilkinson and L. A. Willoughby. Oxford: Clarendon, 1967. Original pub. 1795. 15th Letter.

Shaw, Jeffrey, and Weibel, Peter, eds. *Future Cinema: The Cinematic Imaginary after Film* Cambridge and London: MIT, 2003.

Shayna Maidels. Dir. Lisa M. Kors. 1991.

Taylor, Diana. *The Archive and the Repertoire: Performing Cultural Memory in the Americas.* Durham: Duke Univ., 2003.

Teicholz, Tom. "Einstein in California." *Jewish Journal.com*. Sept. 2, 2004 <http://www.jewishjournal.com/science_and_technology/article/einstein_in_california_20040903/>.

White, Hayden. *The Content of the Form: Narrative Discourse and Historical Representation*. Baltimore and London: Johns Hopkins Univ., 1987.

About the Contributors

LISA ANSELL is Associate Director of the Casden Institute for the Study of the Jewish Role in American Life at the University of Southern California. She received her BA in French and Near East Studies from UCLA and her MA in Middle East Studies from Harvard University. She was the Chair of the World Language Department of New Community Jewish High School for five years before coming to USC in August, 2007.

SHANA BERNSTEIN is Assistant Professor of History at Southwestern University. She received her PhD in US History at Stanford University, and was a Mellon Postdoctoral Fellow at Northwestern University before she joined the faculty at Southwestern. Her manuscript, *Forgotten Coalition: Interracial Civil Rights Activism in World War II and Cold War Los Angeles*, is forthcoming from Oxford University Press.

WILLIAM DEVERELL is Director of the Huntington-USC Institute on California and the West and Professor of History, the University of Southern California.

FRANCES DINKELSPIEL is a fifth-generation Californian who grew up in San Francisco. A graduate of Stanford University and the Columbia University Graduate School of Journalism, Frances spent more than twenty years working as a newspaper reporter. Her freelance work has appeared in the *New York Times*, *Los Angeles Times*, *People Magazine*, and the *San Francisco Chronicle*. She has also taught at the Berkeley Graduate School of Journalism. *Towers of Gold: How One Jewish Immigrant Named Isaias Hellman Created California*, was a *San Francisco Chronicle* bestseller and notable book of 2008.

DAVID EPSTEIN, co-editor of the *Western States Jewish History Journal*, is a graduate of Wesleyan University. He majored in economics and history. He has lectured throughout the country on the history of the Jews of the West. He is also the publisher of *The American Rabbi* journal and website.

MARSHA KINDER is University Professor of Cinematic Arts at the University of Southern California, and Executive Producer and Project Leader of the Labyrinth Project.

GINA NAHAI is a best-selling author, and a professor of Creative Writing at the University of Southern California. Her novels have been translated into eighteen languages, and have been selected as "One of the Best Books of the Year" by the *Los Angeles Times* and the *Chicago Tribune*.

GLADYS STURMAN, co-editor of the *Western States Jewish History Journal*, is a graduate of the University of Judaism (now the American Jewish University), majoring in History. She has been a Jewish community activist in the Los Angeles area for fifty years. She lectures and teaches extensively throughout the area on Jewish topics.

KAREN S. WILSON is a doctoral candidate in US History at the University of California, Los Angeles, expecting to obtain her degree in 2010. Her dissertation project, entitled "On the Cosmopolitan Frontier: Jews in Nineteenth-Century Los Angeles," examines the ways in which social networks shaped the incorporation and distinctiveness of Jewish settlers in post-Gold Rush society. Her research interests center on immigrants to the American West and urbanization in nineteenth-century frontiers and borderlands. She also is serving as curator for an exhibition on the history of Jews in Los Angeles to be mounted at the Autry National Center.

BRUCE ZUCKERMAN is the Myron and Marian Casden Director of the Casden Institute and a Professor of Religion at USC, where he teaches courses in the Hebrew Bible, the Bible in western literature, the ancient Near East, and archaeology. A specialist in photographing and reconstructing ancient texts, he is involved in numerous projects related to the Dead Sea Scrolls. On ancient topics, his major publications are *Job the Silent: A Study in Biblical Counterpoint* and *The Leningrad Codex: A Facsimile Edition*, for which he and his brother Kenneth did the principal photography. Zuckerman also has a continuing interest in modern Jewish thought, often looking at modern issues from an ancient perspective. He most recently co-authored *Double Takes: Thinking and Rethinking Issues of Modern Judaism in Ancient Contexts* with Zev Garber and contributed a chapter to Garber's book, *Mel Gibson's Passion: The Film, the Controversy, and Its Implications*.

The USC Casden Institute for the Study of the Jewish Role in American Life

The American Jewish community has played a vital role in shaping the politics, culture, commerce and multiethnic character of Southern California and the American West. Beginning in the mid-nineteenth century, when entrepreneurs like Isaias Hellman, Levi Strauss and Adolph Sutro first ventured out West, American Jews became a major force in the establishment and development of the budding Western territories. Since 1970, the number of Jews in the West has more than tripled. This dramatic demographic shift has made California—specifically, Los Angeles—home to the second largest Jewish population in the United States. Paralleling this shifting pattern of migration, Jewish voices in the West are today among the most prominent anywhere in the United States. Largely migrating from Eastern Europe, the Middle East and the East Coast of the United States, Jews have invigorated the West, where they exert a considerable presence in every sector of the economy—most notably in the media and the arts. With the emergence of Los Angeles as a world capital in entertainment and communications, the Jewish perspective and experience in the region are being amplified further. From artists and activists to scholars and professionals, Jews are significantly influencing the shape of things to come in the West and across the United States. In recognition of these important demographic and societal changes, in 1998 the University of Southern California established a scholarly institute dedicated to studying contemporary Jewish life in America with special emphasis on the western United States. The Casden Institute explores issues related to the interface between the Jewish community and the broader, multifaceted cultures that form the nation—issues of relationship as much as of Jewishness itself. It is also enhancing the educational experience for students at USC and elsewhere by exposing them to the problems—and promise—of life in Los Angeles' ethnically, socially, culturally and economically diverse community. Scholars, students and community leaders examine the ongoing contributions of American Jews in the arts, business, media, literature, education, politics, law and social relations, as well as the relationships between Jewish Americans and other groups, including African Americans,

Latinos, Asian Americans and Arab Americans. The Casden Institute's scholarly orientation and contemporary focus, combined with its location on the West Coast, set it apart from—and makes it an important complement to—the many excellent Jewish Studies programs across the nation that center on Judaism from an historical or religious perspective.

For more information about the USC Casden Institute,
visit www.usc.edu/casdeninstitute, e-mail casden@usc.edu,
or call (213) 740-3405.

www.ingramcontent.com/pod-product-compliance
Lightning Source LLC
Chambersburg PA
CBHW051944160426
43198CB00013B/2298